CW00688301

Opening up
Amos

MICHAEL BENTLEY

DayOne

Opening up
Amos

MICHAEL BENTLEY

'Michael Bentley is not trying to answer all your questions about Amos, but to raise some! He is 'opening up'—and pulling you into—the book, and he does this with both simplicity and vitality. His study is both convicting (as Amos would want) and stretching (as we have need).'
Dr Dale Ralph Davis
Pastor of Woodland Presbyterian Church, Hattiesberg, Mississippi, formerly Professor of Old Testament at the Reformed Theological Seminary, Jackson, Mississippi, U.S.A., and a well-known commentator on the Old Testament

'It is always a treat to find an author who can 'earth' God's Word in practical application for the Christian life, family and work. Michael Bentley's bent for clear, honest exposition makes this commentary a gem! I particularly liked the natural way in which the reader is exposed to the New Testament through the studies on Amos. A must-read for mature and new Christians alike. Use this for personal study or group study—whichever way, you will not fail to be challenged to a Christ-honouring life.'

Roland Eskinazi
Senior pastor of Goodwood Baptist Church, Cape Town, South Africa

'Those readers who are familiar with Michael Bentley's other commentaries will certainly not be disappointed with this one. He combines his considerable expository and communication skills to produce a helpful and practical guide to the Book of Amos. He vividly portrays the world in which Amos ministered and helpfully applies the book's timeless lessons to present day issues. The questions at the end of each chapter make it ideal for either personal or group study.'

Colin D Jones
Pastor of Three Bridges Free Church, Crawley, England

© Day One Publications 2006

First printed 2006

ISBN 1 84625 041 -2

9 781846 250415

British Library Cataloguing in Publication Data available

Published by Day One Publications

Ryelands Road, Leominster, HR6 8NZ

Telephone 01568 613 740   FAX 01568 611 473

email—sales@dayone.co.uk

web site—www.dayone.co.uk

North American—e-mail-sales@dayonebookstore.com

North American web site—www.dayonebookstore.com

Designed by Steve Devane and printed by Gutenberg Press, Malta

Dedication

To all my friends in South Africa, and especially evangelist Doug Crutchley of Cape Town, who encouraged me to complete this commentary

List of Bible abbreviations

THE OLD TESTAMENT		1 Chr.	1 Chronicles	Dan.	Daniel
		2 Chr.	2 Chronicles	Hosea	Hosea
Gen.	Genesis	Ezra	Ezra	Joel	Joel
Exod.	Exodus	Neh.	Nehemiah	Amos	Amos
Lev.	Leviticus	Esth.	Esther	Obad.	Obadiah
Num.	Numbers	Job	Job	Jonah	Jonah
Deut.	Deuteronomy	Ps.	Psalms	Micah	Micah
Josh.	Joshua	Prov.	Proverbs	Nahum	Nahum
Judg.	Judges	Eccles.	Ecclesiastes	Hab.	Habakkuk
Ruth	Ruth	S.of.S.	Song of Solomon	Zeph.	Zephaniah
1 Sam.	1 Samuel	Isa.	Isaiah	Hag.	Haggai
2 Sam.	2 Samuel	Jer.	Jeremiah	Zech.	Zechariah
1 Kings	1 Kings	Lam.	Lamentations	Mal.	Malachi
2 Kings	2 Kings	Ezek.	Ezekiel		

THE NEW TESTAMENT		Gal.	Galatians	Heb.	Hebrews
		Eph.	Ephesians	James	James
Matt.	Matthew	Phil.	Philippians	1 Peter	1 Peter
Mark	Mark	Col.	Colossians	2 Peter	2 Peter
Luke	Luke	1 Thes.	1 Thessalonians	1 John	1 John
John	John	2 Thes.	2 Thessalonians	2 John	2 John
Acts	Acts	1 Tim.	1 Timothy	3 John	3 John
Rom.	Romans	2 Tim.	2 Timothy	Jude	Jude
1 Cor.	1 Corinthians	Titus	Titus	Rev.	Revelation
2 Cor.	2 Corinthians	Philem.	Philemon		

Overview

When Amos delivered his prophecy the nation of Israel was experiencing a time of great plenty; trade routes passing through the region had brought wealth into the land and, as a consequence, many of the people benefited from the increase in money entering the country—some had grown very rich indeed. These favoured few had become so affluent that they owned two houses—a winter house as well as a summer one (3:15)—and they had very expensive furniture to put in them both (6:4). They possessed beds and couches to lie on (3:12); and they could drink wine by the bowlful and apply the finest lotions to themselves (6:6).

But these things did not necessarily mean that God was shining with favour upon the land. They could not assume that they were prosperous because God was satisfied with them. Their behaviour was deficient in two major ways: many of them were oppressing the poor, and their worship of God was a mere formality. God's prophets had spoken about these kinds of sins, and Amos added to his warning of judgement which was about to come through the invasion of the terrible Assyrians, the dreaded superpower of the Middle East, who lived way to the north of them.

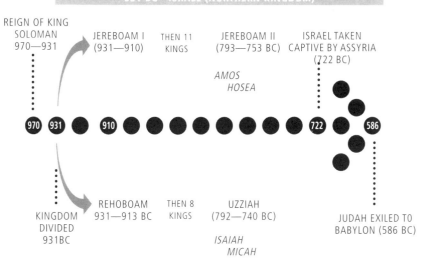

Introduction

According to the first verse of this prophecy, Amos prophesied during the reigns of Uzziah (792-740B.C.) in the southern kingdom of Judah and Jeroboam II (793-753B.C.) in the northern kingdom of Israel. This means that he preached around about 760-750B.C.

G od called him from Judah to travel northwards to warn the Israelites of their coming doom—a judgement which was also to come upon Judah one hundred years later. Although the nations around Israel were sinful, God's major concern in this prophecy was the disobedience of his own people whom he had rescued from the Egyptian slavery.

In this book we will look at the various ways God used to highlight the dangers the people were in. He gives specific details of his judgements on Israel in 3:1-6:14. Five visions occur between 7:1 and 9:10. Interspersed within this section of the prophecy is a gracious call to 'seek me and live' (5:4-5) and the book ends with the promise of great revival (9:11-15).

Background

What are the ideal conditions that go to make up a good life? Are we better off when things are going well for us—when we have plenty of money in the bank, our health and that of our family is excellent and no one is criticizing us? Or are we likely to be happier when life is not so easy?

When all seems to be going well, Christians should not become self-satisfied and careless in their devotion to the Lord. It is then that pride of position and achievements is in danger of taking precedence over all other matters and we are in danger of behaving as though we can manage without God. Before August 2005 the city of New Orleans in the southern states of America no doubt thought of itself as a prosperous city but the force of Hurricane Katrina rapidly smashed all its complacency, and as I write this it still lies in ruins.

The northern kingdom of Israel was smug and contented, so the Lord called this humble man, Amos, to leave his sheep on the Judean hillside and turn his attention to 'the lost sheep of Israel' (see also Matt. 15:24).

Amos did not call himself a prophet. He merely introduces himself as 'one of the shepherds of Tekoa' (1:1). Yet despite his apparent humility, Amos was a prophet, a very powerful one, and his book holds an important place in the Old Testament.

A prophet in the Bible

A prophet was not merely someone who foretold the future; he (or occasionally she) was someone who spoke the word of the Lord. The burden of the message was always to bring the people back to the law which God had given to Moses on Mount Sinai. God had made a covenant (agreement) at that time with the people. He told them that 'if you obey me fully and keep my covenant, then out of all nations you will be my treasured possession' (Exod. 19:5).

This means that all true prophets were required to speak the message of the Lord; they were not just to pass on their own thoughts. This is why we so often find them delivering a twofold message. On the one hand, they warned the people of the curses which would befall all those who disobeyed the covenant; and on the other hand, they spoke warmly of the blessings which would come to those who followed the ways of the Lord (i.e. lived their lives in obedience to God's law). No prophet spoke of any halfway house; everyone was either a covenant-keeper or a covenant-breaker. They were either in a covenant relationship with God because they were attempting to keep the Ten Commandments and the rest of the law—or they were at enmity with him because they refused to obey him and his laws.

The divided kingdom

Following the death of Solomon (some 150 years before the days of Amos), Israel had been divided into two distinct parts; the southern kingdom was called Judah (this included the great city of Jerusalem), and the north section was named Israel (sometimes referred to as Ephraim or Samaria; Samaria was the main city of the northern kingdom). Amos prophesied while Uzziah was on the throne of Judah and Jeroboam II was king of Israel, around about 750B.C.

Most of the Old Testament prophets addressed their words to the southern kingdom of Judah but two prophets, Amos and Hosea, were sent north to Israel. During the time that these two men were calling Israel back to the ways of God, Isaiah and

Micah were also engaged in similar work in the southern kingdom. It is probable that Amos would have known Hosea and it is very likely that Isaiah and Micah were aware of the activities of each other. All of them urged the people to return to the Lord and his ways—and each one warned them of judgement to come.

> All true prophets were required to speak the message of the Lord; they were not just to pass on their own thoughts.

Amos grew up in the southern kingdom; 'Tekoa was a small town about six miles south of Bethlehem and eleven miles from Jerusalem'.[1] This was a very bleak area—almost a wilderness. He would have had a hard life. He would have only been able to make a living through his industrious determination. He would have needed to have been the kind of person who would not easily hold back when presented with a difficult task.

However, on the face of it, Amos was not an influential person. He did not mix with royalty, like Isaiah, nor was he a priest like Jeremiah; he was just an ordinary working herdsman. However, it seems that he was a very successful shepherd and fruit farmer. In Amos 7:14-15 he tells us, 'I was neither a prophet nor a prophet's son, but I was a shepherd, and I also took care of sycamore-fig trees. But the LORD took me from tending the flock and said to me, "Go, prophesy to my people Israel."'

So, even though he was a native of Judah, God sent him to travel to Israel and prophesy specifically to the people of the northern kingdom.

FOR FURTHER STUDY

1. Read Proverbs 30:8. Now notice the way in which the people of Israel were outwardly rich in Amos 3:12,15; 4:1; 6:4,6. Then read 2:6-7; 4:1, 5:10,12; 6:1-6. How did these people and their wives behave?

2. Amos was called to be a prophet while he was about his daily work. What other Bible characters were called to serve the Lord while they were engaged in their ordinary tasks? (See Exod. 3:1-12; 1 Sam. 16:11-13 and Luke 5:1-10.)

TO THINK ABOUT AND DISCUSS

1. Jesus said, 'It is hard for a rich man to enter the kingdom of heaven' (Matt. 19:23). Does this mean that no Christian should have a good bank balance? (See Matt. 6:19-24; 19:16-30.)

2. How should wealthy believers behave with their money? (See Luke 12:33; Luke 16:9; James 5:1-6.)

3. What can Christians learn from the experience of Asaph in Psalm 73?

1 The roar of the enemy

(1:1-2; 3:7-8; 9:1-4)

On 11th September 2001 a man-made disaster changed the modern world. On that day a group of evil terrorists flew two airliners into the Twin Towers of New York.

When that awful thing happened the whole world knew about it—and many people even watched these dreadful events unfolding before their eyes. It is not surprising, then, that a CNN/Time Warner poll taken three months later stated that 73% of those interviewed said, 'It has changed everything for ever.'[2]

I suppose the earthquake mentioned in Amos 1:1 must have had a similar effect on the then known world because the prophet dates 'what he saw concerning Israel' to 'two years before the earthquake.' That destructive earthquake must have etched itself on the memory of the people of the region. It is very likely that the earthquake that the prophet Zechariah refers to many years later (Zech. 14:5) is the same one spoken of here by Amos. For these prophets, the earthquake was a major catastrophe which was long remembered. It also served as a 'divine reinforcement of the words of judgement.'[3]

Amos, being a rather prosperous farmer from Judea, very likely would have had cause to travel northwards into Israel on occasions to sell his produce. While there, he would certainly have observed the ungodly behaviour of the people who claimed to be God's chosen ones. Although he would have known about the sins of Judah (see 2:4), what he saw in Israel appalled him so much that he was compelled by the Lord to speak forcibly about 'what he saw concerning Israel' (1:1).

> Although the Lord Jesus Christ in the humility of his suffering appeared to John like a lamb having been slain, he was also described as 'the Lion of the tribe of Judah' who had 'triumphed' over all of his enemies.

We do not know how old he was when he left Tekoa, but he went with all speed to urge the people of Israel to repent of their iniquity and turn back to the Lord. The burden of his message is summarized in 1:2: 'The LORD roars from Zion and thunders from Jerusalem; the pastures of the shepherds dry up, and the top of Carmel withers.'

'LORD' here is in capital letters. This tells us that the word used is the covenant name for God. The use of this name reminds us, as it did the people of Amos's time, that the Lord has a covenant relationship with his people. He is their maker and their husband (Isa. 54:5) and, if they are faithful to him and his covenant, he is their God.

Amos likens God to one of the most powerful animals in the world. He describes the Lord's voice as 'roaring from Zion'. In the Scriptures the lion is a symbol of sovereignty, strength and courage. Although the Lord Jesus Christ in the humility of his suffering appeared to John like a lamb having been slain, he was also described as 'the Lion of the tribe of Judah' who had 'triumphed' over all of his enemies (see Rev. 5:4-6). So in judgement, the Lord roars from Zion, the place where he dwells in the midst of his people. His roaring is a sign of 'his righteous vengeance against the wickedness of men and nations'.4 We will be hearing the roaring of this 'lion' throughout the whole of Amos's prophecy (see 3:8 and Isa. 31:4).

As a result of the Lord's thunderous voice, 'the pastures of the shepherds dry up, and the top of Carmel withers' (1:2). Mount Carmel is a prominent large hill, surrounded by a plain, and from which constant streams of water often flowed. From such mountain streams the prophet Elijah was sustained through three and a half years of drought (see 1 Kings 17 and 18). But when the Lord came in judgement the pastures, long enjoyed by the shepherds and their charges, would dry up completely as a sign of the Lord's anger against the sin of the people.

For further study ▶

FOR FURTHER STUDY

1. Read the following verses: 1 Kings 19:11-12; Isaiah 29:6; Ezekiel 38:19; Matthew 27:54; 28:2; Acts 16:26; Revelation 6:12; 8:5; 11:13,19; 16:18. What is the significance of the earthquake in each case?

2. Read the blessings of Jacob on his children in Genesis 49:1-27, noticing that he says that Judah is a 'lion's cub' and that 'the sceptre will not depart from Judah' (Gen. 49:9-10). Look up the following verses: Numbers 24:9; Ezekiel 19:1-7; Micah 5:8. Note that Judah (or Israel) is often pictured as a lion. Then see how this figure of a lion is applied to the Lord Jesus Christ in Revelation 5:5.

TO THINK ABOUT AND DISCUSS

1. Think back to some occasion or period in your life when you were faced with a dreadful incident which you consider may have been the Lord warning you to mend your ways. What have you learned from this experience? How have your thinking and behaviour changed as a result?

2. When people fail to listen to the warnings of the gospel, how should we react? (See Exod. 32:32; 2 Tim. 4:2.)

2 God's judgements against surrounding nations

(1:3-2:3)

The voice of God, through his servant Amos, now begins to 'roar'. First of all he cries out with great ferocity against the nations near to Israel. Then he takes his hearers (and readers) on an imaginary tour of the surrounding geographical area, moving in a decreasing spiral of shame until, in 2:4-16, he reaches Israel itself and speaks about their complacency.

He starts by warning of impending judgement on Israel's neighbour which lay to the north, Damascus, the capital of Syria (1:3-5); then he travels to their neighbour, Gaza, the home of the Philistines (1:6-8). From there he journeys back towards Tyre, the abode of the once-powerful Phoenicians (1:9-10), and then goes to Edom, the home of a proud mountainous people (1:11-12). He continues to move in a circular motion until he arrives at Ammon (1:13-15) which is almost directly north of Edom. Finally, he moves a little way to the south again until he reaches Moab, the country which had been the home of godly Ruth (2:1-3).

God's warning to each one of these kingdoms is very similar; he condemns them. You will see that the opening words to each of these nations are: 'This is what the LORD says: "For three sins ... even for four"' (1:3, 6, 9, 11, 13 and 2:1). No one could be in any doubt in reading these words that these various peoples were going to be judged by God because of their many sins. While even one sin is abominable to God, they were not going to be chastened merely because of one, or even two sins—they were guilty of a huge quantity of evil, which he describes as 'three sins ... even four'.

Why does God use this formula to describe the many sins of these nations? Some people suggest that the Lord speaks of 'three and four sins' because three plus four equals seven, which is the number of completeness. Whether that is so or not, it is true that these people were completely wicked in their behaviour towards others. Gordon Keddie puts it like this: 'God is measuring human wickedness and there will be a reckoning and absolute justice will be served.'[5]

After each nation is denounced the Lord then states categorically, 'I will not turn back my wrath'. In other words, because of the intensity and persistence of these people's sins, nothing will be able to divert God from his determination to utterly destroy these nations and their communities. This is one of the persistent themes of the whole Bible; sin must be punished because it is an abomination to the Lord. One of the many places where we can read about this is in Ezekiel 18:4 where the prophet declares, 'The soul who sins is the one who will die'.

As we are taken to each of these nations in turn we see that there is no evidence that any of them were ashamed of their evil ways. Not one of them is prepared to repent of their sin, nor do they have any desire to turn from it.

Damascus (1:3-5)

God denounces Syria (whose capital city is Damascus) because she had committed awful atrocities against the people of Gilead, which was in the northern part of Israel. There was constant war between Damascus and Israel, and during these times the people of Damascus had inflicted great brutality (see 2 Kings 10:32-33 and 13:22). When Amos described the sins of Damascus as threshing 'Gilead with sledges having iron teeth', he was saying that they had torn the people of the northern area of Israel apart in much the same way as the sharp teeth on agricultural threshing implements tear the heads of grain from their stalks.

Because of this their punishment will be like fire burning them up. The people of Syria will be punished by the destruction of all their palaces and pleasant places of recreation (i.e. the places frequented by Hazael, the king of Syria). The self-important Syrians, who had power in the Valley of Aven and in Beth Eden, would be scattered and flee far away to Kir (which location is unknown today) from where they had originated (see 9:7).

Gaza (1:6-9)

The people of Philistia (Gaza) who lived along the southern

coastline, guarding the road which led up from Egypt, were also to be punished for their sins. The Philistines had been a continual 'thorn in the sides' of the children of Israel as they had sought to establish themselves in the land during the time of King Saul and King David.

In the days preceding those of Amos, these same people had '[taken] captive whole communities and sold them to Edom'. They had done this for gain (as had the people of Tyre—see 1:9). Edom had long been the enemy of Israel (see below). Because of their sin, each of the local leaders of the Philistines, the kings of Ashdod, Ashkelon and Ekron, were going to be destroyed. This prophecy is echoed in Zephaniah 2:4-7.

Tyre (1:9-10)

Tyre was chief city of splendid Phoenicia, which had been one of the leading seafaring nations of the past. In 1 Kings 5:1 and 12 we read that the king of Tyre and King Solomon had made a treaty of friendship. But selfishly the people of Tyre had broken their agreement and had sold slaves to their enemy (Edom). God takes a very dim view of covenant-breakers, therefore he is going to destroy Tyre and all its great wealth.

Edom (1:11-12)

Edom was a nation set up high on the rocks to the south of the region. Their territory guarded the south-west entry into the Promised Land. When Moses arrived at Kadesh (having travelled through the desert for many years) he asked the king of Edom for permission to pass through his land. This consent ought to have been given readily and cheerfully because the Edomites were descended from Jacob's brother, Esau, but it was rudely and vigorously refused (Num. 20:14-21). This set up a stream of hostility which continued throughout the generations until the time of Amos.

We have already had hints about the cruelty of these people because they purchased slaves from Gaza and from Tyre (see above). Because of their sinful behaviour God was going to destroy their main cities of Teman and Bozrah; and with them, the power of the people would disappear.

Ammon (1:13-15)

We have noted that Edom was descended from Esau; Ammon's father was Lot. These people did not have a promising beginning because they sprang from the incestuous relationship between Lot and his two daughters (Gen. 19:30-38). As time went by, things became even worse.

Like Edom, the people had little compassion and were even prepared to murder whole populations, including mothers and their unborn babies. They too, had 'stifled' all possible attitudes of kindness in their selfish desires to extend their borders. Their main concern was to increase their power in the area. But God's judgement was going to fall on these people too, and they and their leaders would be taken away into exile.

Moab (2:1-3)

Moab lay between Ammon (to the north) and Edom (to the south). The Lord's chief complaint against this people was that they desecrated the bodies of their enemies. Instead of giving the king of Edom a decent burial, they had burned his bones, grinding them to powder, perhaps to use as mortar for their building work. We can be sure that the people of Moab were guilty of many other sins as well.

> It may well have been that the people of Israel were filled with a smugness when they heard Amos warning these other nations of God's wrath against them. They, like us, no doubt found that it is very easy to gloat over the misfortunes of our enemies.

Even though Edom was the persistent enemy of Israel and Judah, God would not sanction any disrespect towards the body of a dead person—be it of a king or a commoner. And for this reason he says that he will 'send fire upon Moab that will consume the fortresses of Kerioth' (their chief city or perhaps group of cities). Just as they burned the body of Edom's king, so they themselves would be consumed by the fire of God's judgement.

It may well have been that the people of Israel were filled with a smugness when they heard Amos warning these other nations of God's wrath against them. They, like us, no doubt found that it is very easy to gloat over the misfortunes of our enemies. However, if this was the case then God's people were being very foolish because their turn to feel the sting of God's tongue would come to them before long.

FOR FURTHER STUDY

1. Read Habakkuk 1:13; why is God unable to look on evil and tolerate any wrongdoing? Read Revelation 21-22; how is the beauty and glory of heaven described? Not even one sin is to be allowed into the presence of God. How can people be freed from their sin? (See 1 John 1:7b.)

2. Read Obadiah 10-14; how did Edom show an attitude of superiority over Jerusalem and its inhabitants?

3. Read the story of Ruth. What significance did this girl from Moab have in Old Testament history? (See Ruth 4:13-22).

TO THINK ABOUT AND DISCUSS

1. The nations surrounding Israel appeared to be unaware that they were offending the Lord because of their sinful ways. Why should we bother to warn our fellow human beings of the danger of God's judgement upon them because of their sin? (See Ezek. 18:4,20; 33:2-6.)

2. The leaders of the surrounding nations behaved in a very haughty way towards God's people. How should Christian leaders exercise their authority over those whom God has put in their charge? (See Ezek. 34:1-10; Acts 20:28-31; 1 Tim. 3:1-13; 1 Peter 5:2-4.)

3. What does God say about the way Christians should treat their bodies? (See Prov. 3:7-8; 1 Cor. 6:19-20; Eph. 5:29.)

3 God's judgements on Judah and Israel

(2:4-16)

We can imagine Amos's audience (the northern kingdom of Israel) nodding their heads in smug agreement as they heard each one of their ungodly neighbours being denounced. It must have been gratifying for them to know that, at last, these nations were going to be punished for some of the dreadful things they had done—particularly for those atrocities they had inflicted on the Israelites.

Yet, as the 'noose of God's judgement'[6] began to tighten around the neck of the southern kingdom of Judah, the people of Israel might well have begun to feel slightly anxious.

Judah (2:4-5)

Even though Judah was part of God's chosen people, they were suffering the same condemnation as the heathen nations: 'For three sins of Judah, even for four, I will not turn back my wrath.'

The charge against Judah is one of the shortest of these eight oracles found in the opening chapters of Amos—and is the only one which fails to mention any sin against humanity. Despite this, there is nothing for Judah to be proud about because their censure is far, far worse. They, who ought to have known better, had 'rejected the law of the LORD and have not kept his decrees'.

Judah, like Israel, had been given the law of the Lord and they had promised to keep it (see Exod. 24:7). They had entered into a covenant relationship with their God and had been bound by that agreement. Their obligation was to serve the Lord alone. Yet despite the deliverance that he had granted them, and the support he had given them during their conquest and settlement in the Promised Land, they had departed from God's word; they had actually 'rejected the law of the LORD'.

They had cast off the law of the Lord by listening to lies (see NIV footnote). These lies had led them to believe that they would find their religion to be more satisfying if they worshipped a god that they could see with their eyes. They behaved as their ancestors had done when they grew tired of having God's appointed judges to rule over them. When Samuel was old the people had wanted a king, 'such as all the other nations have' (1 Sam. 8:5), showing how they had become dissatisfied with the provision God had made for them; they had wanted to be like the other nations. The lie is this: 'It is better to walk by sight than by faith'.

Throughout Judah and Israel's history they had continually turned their backs upon God and his law. This law, given to Moses at Sinai, said that the people should serve only the Lord and not make for themselves any idol to bow down to and worship (Exod. 20:1-6). Such gods were not real and had no power, nevertheless the Israelites did bow down to them and worship them. This showed that they had 'been led astray by false gods, the gods their ancestors followed' (v.4).

The effect of this would be that they would come under God's judgement—a very similar judgement to that which would fall upon the surrounding heathen nations. Fire would come upon the fortresses of Jerusalem. Even that once-blessed place would come under the severe displeasure of God and be ransacked. This shows us that the Lord considered that disloyalty to him and disobedience to the covenant he had made with them in the past are just as serious as the crimes of inhumanity committed by some of the other nations.

Although Amos's prophecy was given to the northern nation of Israel, we should remember that his home was in the southern kingdom—whose destruction he was prophesying in verses 4-5. Surely, then, his heart must have been heavy as he uttered these words about his beloved city of Jerusalem. The blessing for Amos was that he did not live long enough to see the desecration of this blessed city. It was not attacked until many years later—in 586B.C.

Israel (2:6-16)

God is angry with Israel because of her many sins but Amos makes no mention of the Israelites failing to keep his law (as he had to the people of Judah). He did not need to highlight it; their behaviour showed that in this respect, they were just as guilty as the people of the southern kingdom.

The prophet speaks, first of all, about the behaviour of their judges: 'They sell the righteous for silver, and the needy for a pair of sandals' (v.6). Those who were rich behaved as they wanted to, without being questioned; silver passed hands and the corrupt judges convicted those who were innocent, 'the righteous'. It was totally different for the poor. The judges were willing to sell a poor man into slavery—even though his debt might have been as small as the cost of a cheap pair of sandals—because the creditor paid him part of the money he received from the sale.

We can almost hear the sadness in God's voice as, through Amos, the Lord speaks out about the lack of compassion shown by the rich people of Israel for the plight of their poor fellow countrymen. The rich and clever in Israel treated the poor like dirt and denied them justice because they were not wealthy enough to bribe the judges (v.7).

> We can almost hear the sadness in God's voice as, through Amos, the Lord speaks out about the lack of compassion shown by the rich people of Israel for the plight of their poor fellow countrymen.

Then the prophet quickly moves on to another way in which the Israelites failed to keep God's law: 'Father and son use the same girl and so profane my holy name. They lie down beside every altar on garments taken in pledge. In the house of their god they drink wine taken as fines' (vv.7-8). It is unlikely that 'the same girl' was the wife of the father and therefore the son's mother; this was forbidden in Leviticus 20:11 on pain of death. It may refer to fathers and sons consorting with prostitutes, but could also refer to the 'holy' women who were dedicated to Baal. The economy of the whole area depended on successful agricultural production. In an attempt to achieve abundant fruitfulness, the Canaanites 'acted out' fertility rites in the temples of their gods. Even though the Israelites were forbidden to follow the heathen religion around them, it seems that many of their farmers were eager to indulge their lustful natures by entering into sexual union with these women—all in the name of religion!

To support this view we see that one of the specific things for which God condemns them is that they had also partaken in religious ceremonies by lying down beside 'every altar' (perhaps with a girl) in the house of (heathen) gods. The Lord is therefore denouncing the people not only for sexual immorality, but also for consorting with heathen women in the framework of heathen worship.

> Things are no different today. It is amazing that now those who are caught in sinful acts will readily explain away their behaviour—even to the point of saying 'in my case this is not sinful'.

Things are no different today. It is amazing that now those who are caught in sinful acts will readily explain away their behaviour—even to the point of saying 'in my case this is not sinful'.

Not only had the people indulged in iniquity, they had also abused the underprivileged by wrapping themselves in 'garments taken in pledge' from the poor. Exodus 22:26 and Deuteronomy 24:12-13 make it clear that clothing should have been returned to the poor by nightfall. In addition to this, they used the money extorted from the poor to go on 'drinking sprees': they had 'caroused with wine exacted from the people by unjust fines'.7

From verses 9 to 12 Amos reminds them of some important periods of their history. God had 'destroyed the Amorite (the Canaanites) before them'. Even though the nations were very strong and powerful, the Lord not only destroyed their work (their 'fruit above'), he had also taken steps to prevent them from re-emerging ('his roots below'). Next he pointed out his great act of deliverance in bringing them out of the awful slavery of Egypt. This was in stark contrast to the way in which they were behaving; they had sold—enslaved—'the righteous for silver' (v.6). Not only had he delivered them from the bondage of Egypt, he had led them for forty years in the desert and given them the land of the Amorites.

The Israelites were no doubt still very grateful to the Lord for this goodness to them, but they were not so pleased by the next two groups of people that Amos mentioned. God had 'raised up prophets from among [their] sons and Nazirites from among [their] young men.' To emphasize the importance of this, God then asks them, 'Is this not true, people of Israel?' (v.11).

It seems that by the time of Amos, the holy life of the Nazirites had been abandoned. Numbers 6:1-6 tells us that

Nazirites had to refrain from imbibing strong drink and their hair had to remain uncut. Perhaps these practices had been an embarrassment to the people because they highlighted their own bad behaviour: apparently the Israelites had tried to force the Nazirites to 'drink wine and [had] commanded the prophets not to prophesy' (v.12).

These same sins are illustrated in the New Testament. The Lord Jesus Christ wept over Jerusalem because the people killed the prophets and stoned those sent there (Matt. 23:37) and Paul warned the early church that men would continue to 'arise and distort the truth in order to draw away disciples after them' (Acts 20:30).

In verses 13-16 Amos gives a very vivid description of the punishment which will come upon disobedient Israel. They will be crushed (not merely bruised) 'as a cart crushes when loaded with grain'. There will be no escape for the swift runners, the strong, the warriors, the archers, the fleet-footed soldiers, the horsemen or the bravest warriors. They will go, naked, out of existence on 'that day' when the Lord comes in divine judgement upon them. In fact, that day did arrive, and Israel was taken away by the Assyrians, never to be heard of again.

However, with every warning of coming judgement there is always a call to repentance, whether specifically spoken, or, as here, merely implied. Isaiah prophesied, 'Give ear and come to me; hear me, that your soul may live' (Isa. 55:3). Yet these stubborn people continually refused to listen to the voice of the Lord's prophet because they did not like what they heard. They did not want to be challenged or shaken out of their comfortable lifestyle.

Still today individuals ignore God's warnings. They think that it is all right to follow the conventions of the society in which they live, even when these contravene God's Word. But we can easily see the danger in this kind of thinking: those who allow the activities of this world to intrude too much into their lives will discover that these things choke them and they produce no fruit for God's glory (see Matt. 13:22).

> Even those sound evangelical churches where the pure Word of God is faithfully preached can become guilty of merely listening to God's Word but not doing 'what it says' (James 1:23).

Churches, too, are tempted to adopt practices which ignore the clear teaching of God's Word, but if they yield they will soon fall away from the gospel message. Even those sound evangelical churches where the pure Word of God is faithfully preached can become guilty of merely listening to God's Word but not doing 'what it says' (James 1:23). Sadly, people are 'moving the goalposts' in the Bible to fit in with their lives.

For further study ▶

34

FOR FURTHER STUDY

1. Read 2 Kings 17:13-21; what were the consequences of Israel and Judah's failure to keep God's commands and honour the covenant he had made with them?

2. Israel itself came under the condemnation of the Lord and 1 Peter 4:17 tells us that judgement begins 'with the family of God'. What are some of the consequences for those who do 'not obey the gospel of God' (see Matt. 25:31-46; 2 Thes. 1:8-9)?

3. In Jesus's Parable of the Tenants (Mark 12:1-12) we are told about the tenants who refused to give the owner of the vineyard his rightful share of the fruit. Notice how their disobedience to the servants eventually led to the murder of the owner's son. What does this parable tell us about the way people react to the prophets and Jesus Christ?

TO THINK ABOUT AND DISCUSS

1. Why do people turn away from God, when he is the only one who is able to save completely? (See Jer. 13:22-23 and Rom. 1:25.)

2. Jeremiah 2:13 speaks of two great sins.

(a) What are some of the ways in which born-again Christian people can forsake him who is 'the spring of living water'?

(b) What kind of things do we use to help ourselves, rather than putting our trust in God alone?

3. What are some of the ways in which nations have shunned the Word of God today?

4 Questions that demand an answer

(3:1-8)

As Amos gets further into the urgency of his message, he cries out, 'Hear this word the LORD has spoken' (v.1). This is a grave message of warning.

God's chosen people (3:1-2)

For many years Israel (and Judah) had been relaxing in comparative peace and prosperity, so they must have been very startled to hear Amos declare 'Hear this word the LORD has spoken against you, O people of Israel—against the whole family I brought up out of Egypt'.

The people of Israel had often rested on the fact that they were the only nation that the Lord had 'chosen' (v.2); they were extra-special. The word 'chosen' in the NIV is often translated 'known' (e.g. NKJV and ESV). To know someone in this sense was an indication of a very close relationship—like that of a man and woman in marriage. The AV translation of Genesis 4:1 says, 'Adam knew Eve his wife; and she conceived, and bare Cain'.

In this prophecy, God was not just addressing the northern kingdom; he spoke of the 'whole family I brought up out of Egypt'. Although the Israelites had been split into two nations for a long while, God still saw them as one people.

But privileges go hand-in-hand with responsibilities. We have already seen some of the sins of Israel described in lurid detail. Now, as the Lord highlights his choice of the people we can see how ungrateful they were, especially in view of God's goodness to them.

> ...a person's 'walk'. This is a term that is often used in the Bible to describe someone's whole manner of life—their desires and their actions. Christians should be people who delight to 'walk with God.'

Verse 3 speaks about a person's 'walk'. This is a term that is often used in the Bible to describe someone's whole manner of life—their desires and their actions. Christians should be people who delight to 'walk with God.' They ought to have a close and continuous relationship with their Lord. They should love him and his words and be eager to obey his commands.

The Lord had called Amos to speak to the people so that they would come to their senses and repent, yet he seems not to have made very much impression on them, because most of them had failed to mend their ways. Israel was continuing to live under the delusion that because God had chosen and loved them, he would protect them to the end of their days—regardless of their behaviour.

However, the next words of Amos must surely have shaken them out of their complacency. The prophet continues, 'Therefore, [because I have chosen you of all the families of the earth] I will punish you for all your sins' (v.2).

Telling questions (3:3-6)

Amos asks the people a rapid series of illuminating questions—the first of which is, 'Do two walk together unless they have agreed to do so?' (v.3b). The answer he expects is obviously, 'No'. When two people go for a walk they have to agree the purpose of their walk and the time and place they will meet.

It was clear to Amos that Israel was not 'walking with God'; they had broken their agreement (their covenant) with the Lord. However, Amos was walking with God (see v.7) and his close relationship to the Lord meant that God's immediate plan for Israel had been made known to him. The prophet now proceeds to warn Israel of the danger they are in, and he does this by asking them questions which can easily be understood.

Three pairs of questions

Each pair of questions signifies 'cause' and 'effect', or 'warning' and 'consequence'.

1. For his first pair of questions Amos again uses the figure of a lion (see 1:2; 3:8 and also Isa. 31:4). He asks, 'Does a lion roar in the thicket when he has no prey?' No. A hungry lion, seeking food, will make no sound while stalking his prey, but the moment he starts to pounce upon the unfortunate animal he utters a triumphant roar.

Think about this, Israel, says Amos. The time of roaring is fast approaching. The lion would not roar while in the thicket (his hiding place) if he had no prey, but soon the Lord will bring judgement upon his people (through Assyria) and then he will be growling in his den because the punishment is being brought to bear upon Israel. Spiritually this symbolizes God's satisfaction (his justice) that the sins of his people are about to be atoned for.

2. In the second pair of questions Israel is seen as a flighty bird. Birds of prey are always on the lookout for food. When this bird sees something that 'takes his eye' he swoops down in his selfish desire, only to discover, too late, that he has flown into a trap. Certainly the trap (Israel's punishment) would not come into play if the people had not been tempted by it. Sin had caused God's people to be so complacent that they were off guard. They had yielded to temptation, and they were to discover that one day they would be caught by God's judgement upon them.

In the second question of this pair we see Israel actually being caught 'red-handed'.[8] The trap would not have been sprung if there had been nothing to catch. But Israel was going to be caught because the people had sinned over and over again. They were just like a bird who is so tempted by a juicy morsel (of sin) that he throws aside all caution and concern for the consequences of his action.

3. Finally Amos uses the figure of a city about to be attacked. Someone (a true prophet of the Lord) sounds a warning trumpet—the call to repentance—designed to put the citizens on the alert. It is a foolish person who takes no precautions when an alarm is sounded; but Israel made no

attempt to take avoiding action when the prophets gave warning of God's impending judgement. Sadly, in Amos's day, the people refused to 'tremble'. They were stupidly complacent; and they refused to believe that 'when disaster comes to a city', the Lord has caused it.

The voice of the prophet (3:7-8)

Lest anyone should question the authority of Amos to speak in such tones to them, he gives this testimony: 'Surely the Sovereign LORD does nothing without revealing his plan to his servants the prophets' (v.7).

Amos had such a close relationship with his God that he knew what the Lord intended him to say to the people. At the very beginning of this prophecy he declares, 'The words of Amos.' He is not being boastful in saying this. He is merely indicating that his relationship with his God is so rich and so intimate that he knows God's plan. He speaks his own words, yet they are truly God's words.

> Because Amos was a true prophet of the Lord he could not keep silent, even though his message was not an easy one to give. He had to prophesy because he revered God's word, but he also had a deep concern for the people.

Jeremiah speaks in similar terms in Jeremiah 23:18 and 22, warning the people that the words of the false prophets are useless. It is only the true prophet, like himself, who 'has stood in the council of the LORD' and 'listened and heard [God's] word' who can speak God's message. Those who 'listen and hear God's word' can pass it on to others.

Because Amos was a true prophet of the Lord he could not keep silent, even though his message was not an easy one to give. He had to prophesy because he revered God's word, but he also had a deep concern for the people. 'The lion has roared' (v.8); can Israel not hear the sound of approaching danger? Will they not repent of their sins and turn again to the Lord and seek his forgiveness? And surely anyone who perceives the approach of an invading enemy would want to plead with those who have stopped their ears to the warnings that have been uttered.

FOR FURTHER STUDY

1. In Exodus 19:5 we read of God's choice of Israel as his 'treasured possession'. Read Exodus 19:5-6: what were the blessings promised to Israel? What were the things that they were required to do? In what ways had Israel failed to do these things in Amos's time?

2. Look up the following passages: 2 Corinthians 5:7; Galatians 5:16; Ephesians 4:1-2; 5:2,8; Colossians 2:6-7. What does it mean to 'walk with God'?

3. What punishment awaits those who remain unrepentant of their sins? (See Matt. 23:33 and 2 Peter 2:4-9.)

4. God's plan for his people is seen more clearly in the New Testament. How can sinful people escape the judgement of hell? (See Rom. 2:1-4; Heb. 2:1-4.)

TO THINK ABOUT AND DISCUSS

1. In what ways are Christians today like the people of ancient Israel? (See James 4:10 and 1 Peter 5:8-9.)

2. Christians are required to walk humbly with their God. How do the pressures of modern life divert us from this?

3. What warnings are there to be seen today of coming judgement from God? (See e.g. 2 Tim. 3:1-9.)

5 Opulence destroyed

(3:9-15)

The possession of great riches can very easily become a snare. The leading people of Samaria were very wealthy, in huge contrast to the many ordinary people who lived in poverty. One of the reasons for their downfall was that they trusted in their wealth instead of in the Lord

Their double punishment (3:9-10)

Here God details the various ways in which he will punish Israel for their disobedience and he uses very strong words to make his point. In verse 9 he demands, 'Proclaim', and in verse 13 he urges, 'Hear this and testify'. When God speaks, everyone needs to sit up and take notice.

We have already seen that the Lord had warned Israel that punishment would come upon them. Now we see that not only would their chastisement be painful; it would also be insulting. Up until this time in their history, two neighbouring states had been their enemies—Egypt (where their forefathers had been held captive for 400 years) and Philistia (a nation which had constantly harassed Israel throughout the reigns of King Saul and King David). These were nations to whom Israel ought to have borne witness concerning the righteousness of God, yet both of these 'now become witnesses of her apostasy!'9

So we can imagine how uncomfortable the people of Israel felt when Amos spoke this oracle. Just as a child feels doubly offended if his or her feared bully in the playground knows that he or she has been caught doing wrong and is going to be punished for it, so the people of Israel were going to experience great embarrassment as their enemies watched while God brought severe punishment upon them.

> Just as a child feels doubly offended if his or her feared bully in the playground knows that he or she has been caught doing wrong and is going to be punished for it, so the people of Israel were going to experience great embarrassment as their enemies watched while God brought severe punishment upon them.

Three times the word 'fortress' is mentioned in these two verses. These were castles or strongholds where citizens could gather and feel secure from the attacks of their enemies. God addresses the people who reside in the fortresses of the powerful cities of Egypt and Ashdod. He calls upon them to observe the great unrest that is within

Israel. What is the cause of this unrest? It is the gradual awareness that God means business; the God who has done so much for his own people (vv.1-2) is actually going to turn against them. They had assumed that they were safe in their strongly fortified cities, but now they begin to realize that even these will not protect them against the Lord's anger.

> They had been sheltering under the physical fortifications of their land, and had also believed that they had security in their riches. This was because much of their wealth was protected by their strong city walls.

They had been sheltering under the physical fortifications of their land, and had also believed that they had security in their riches. This was because much of their wealth was protected by their strong city walls (v.10b). However, God was not going to punish them just because they had wealth; he was going to chastise them because these riches were ill-gained plunder. They had taken these things from the poor through oppression (v.9b) and looting (v.10b), so God declares, 'They do not know how to do right' (v.10a). Their selfishness was the effect of their sin.

Of all people, those who have been delivered from the bondage of their sin should know how to do the right thing. They should have a sense of 'fair play' so that honesty, justice and goodness come to them automatically, but these people had become so greedy that their consciences had been dulled and they had committed the sins of verse 10.

The effects of their enemy (3:11-12)

Just as the people of Samaria had been insensitive to the needs of the poor, so their enemy would come and 'pull down [their] strongholds'. These fortresses, on which they had placed so much reliance, would quickly be destroyed. Israel had built strongholds to protect themselves and their riches but when these were demolished the enemy would plunder their ill-gotten gains. It is as though God was saying, 'You foolishly ignore the preaching of the prophets (even though I have sent them), but you will pay attention to the swords of your heathen conquerors!'[10]

Amos then reminds his hearers/readers of God's law in Exodus 22:12-13 which concerns a man who looks after his neighbour's sheep. If this sheep was killed by a wild animal, the borrower had to bring the remains of the animal to its owner to prove that the animal had been killed and not stolen by him or someone else. God uses this law to give one small glimmer of hope amid his pronouncements of doom upon Israel. They were going to be destroyed by the enemy, yet a very small remnant would remain ('two leg bones or a piece of an ear', v.12). The rest of the verse says the same thing but in a more colourful way. God speaks of 'the edge of their beds' and 'their couches'. The things that will remain for the people of God are not those connected with the worship of the Lord or even participation in heathen ritual, but merely things which speak of sensuality, idleness and bodily care.

Their places of security will be demolished (3:13-15)

Once again Amos calls upon the nations around Israel to 'Hear this'. God is going to 'testify against the house of Jacob'; and for the first time he uses the full might and power of his name, 'The Lord, the LORD God Almighty'. 'He shows that he is the divine warrior' and that 'when he fights against his enemies, he has the power to destroy everything'.[11] Even though they were God's chosen people (v.2), they were not to behave as though they could do whatever they liked.

When we are saved by the precious blood of Christ, we are saved for all eternity and no one can snatch us out of God's hand (John 10:28), but that does not mean that we can ignore God's commandments. We are constantly urged to be holy in all we do (1 Peter 1:15) and to do good works (Eph. 2:10).

God now talks about 'the day' (v.14). This is a regular feature of the prophets in regard to specific events and, particularly, judgements. Amos tells the people about the destruction of the 'things' in which they have placed their hope. First of all, he speaks about religious 'things'— especially 'the altars of Bethel'. To discourage the people of the northern kingdom from going down to Jerusalem (in Judah) to offer sacrifices to God, Jeroboam I had built altars at both ends of his kingdom, at Bethel and at Dan (1 Kings 12:32). Ever since then the people had been placing great faith in their nearest altar (and the one at Bethel is mentioned most frequently). The Israelites believed that they could find refuge by clinging to the horns of that altar if they had accidentally committed a crime—just as could happen at the altar in Jerusalem (see 1 Kings 1:50-53; 2:28-34).

But, God declared, 'On the day I punish Israel for her sins, I will destroy the altars of Bethel; the horns of the altar will be cut off and fall to the ground.' These rich, self-righteous Israelites would discover that it would be useless for them to seek to find security in these man-made altars; not only would the horns be cut off so that they would not be able to cling to them, but the altars themselves would be destroyed. God would show his anger at these false altars.

Secondly, the Lord was going to 'tear down' their comfortable houses. This might be through military force (vv.11-12) or a natural disaster such as an earthquake (2:13; 8:8; 9:1).

The wealthy people of the northern kingdom were boastful. They showed their riches by their vast houses. Perhaps some had winter houses which were in well sheltered parts of the land and also summer houses which were specially built so that they provided cool shade from the blazing sun. These houses were decorated with ivory. Through the destruction of these houses the people would not only be deprived of comfortable homes to live in, but their high status in the land would be diminished.

The chapter ends with the words, 'declares the LORD'; it is God's solemn announcement that he is sending total obliteration upon them.

For further study ▶

FOR FURTHER STUDY

1. How had Egypt oppressed the forefathers of the Israelites (see Exod. 1:8-14; 3:7; 5:4-9 and Heb. 11:26), and how had the Philistines harassed Israel (see 1 Sam. 13:23-14:14; 17:1-58; 2 Sam. 5:17-25; 2 Kings 18:8)?

2. Look up the number of times that the northern kingdom of Israel is referred to as Jacob (Amos 6:8; 7:2 and 5; 8:7). Why is this?

3. What kind of lives are Christians called to live? (See Isa. 35:8; 1 Thes. 4:7; 1 John 3:3.)

TO THINK ABOUT AND DISCUSS

1. What effect does it have on others when Christians fail to behave in right ways? (See 1 Tim. 4:2; Hab. 2:6-11.)

2. What are some of the ways in which people seek comfort in religion? Why is it that special religious clothing and objects cannot save us from God's punishment on sin (see 1 Sam. 15:22; Ps. 51:16-17; Mark 12:33)?

3. Where is the only place to find eternal security? (See Ps. 20:7; 131:1-3; Hab. 3:17-19.)

6 Offending God's holiness

(4:1-5)

'He was a real English gentleman', the bereaved lady said to me about her deceased husband. She meant that he was cultured and always behaved with honesty and kindness. The word 'lady' likewise carries with it an expectation of a certain lifestyle. When someone says, 'She's a lady', they mean that a woman is gracious, hard-working, and lovely in every way.

Self-centred wives (4:1)

However, when we come to Amos 4 we find Amos referring to well-off women in a different tone of voice. He calls them 'you cows of Bashan on Mount Samaria.' These women were utterly materialistic; 'they never stopped chewing the cud of luxury'.[12] Furthermore, they failed to accept any responsibility to care for those who were less privileged than themselves. On the contrary, they 'oppress[ed] the poor and crush[ed] the needy.' It seems that their sole aim was to live a lavish lifestyle.

Isaiah 58:6-7 tells us that God's people should share their food 'with the hungry and ... provide the poor wanderer with shelter', and Jesus himself identified with the hungry and naked (Matt. 25:35-36), but these women in the days of Amos seemed to have no concern for the poor in their society. So Amos calls them 'cows of Bashan'. This sounds like a very rude way of speaking but the Lord was not stooping to indulge in name-calling. He was merely emphasizing the pampered, selfish, ungodly personality of these wealthy women, because Bashan was a very fertile plain the other side of the Jordan River. The very best breed of cattle was farmed there. The cows of Bashan were well-fed and fat.

> It seems that the only thing these uncaring women wanted to do was to 'drink themselves silly' to relieve the boredom of their empty lives.

It seems that these Samaritan women had everything their hearts desired including beautiful, comfortable houses to live in— both in the winter and in the summer (3:15). But unlike real ladies they oppressed the poor and crushed the needy by their selfish behaviour, and treated their husbands as their servants. Amos gives us a flavour of the way they spoke to their husbands—'Bring us some drinks!' It seems that the only thing these uncaring women wanted to do was to 'drink themselves silly' to relieve the boredom of their empty lives.

It is not surprising then, that Amos tells the people of

judgement which 'the Sovereign Lord has sworn by his holiness'. This is a very solemn oath given by the Lord, and it is because of their actions and desires which offend against his holiness.

Deportation again stated (4:2-3)

The prophet has already laid down his main message about their judgement, but now he gives further details of what will happen. Their punishment will be deportation and this is described in graphic detail. It is not just a possibility, nor even a probability, that they will be taken away from their land. God says, 'The time will surely come when you will be taken away with hooks, the last of you with fish-hooks.'

So, having described the rich women as cows, he now speaks about all of the Samaritans as fish who are waiting to be caught by the hooks of the Assyrians. Although the pictures are rather obscure, the meaning is clear. The people of Samaria are going to be expelled from their land. We do not know exactly what is meant by these fish-hooks but a 'few Assyrian reliefs picturing captives being marched into exile by means of a ring through their nose or lip'[13] have been found by archaeologists. This is a fitting punishment for them, considering their 'superior behaviour'. In their days of prosperity they had treated the ordinary people as animals; shortly they would be dealt with in a similar way themselves.

In verse 3 we read about 'breaks in the [city] wall', either broken down by an enemy or by an earthquake. Whatever is going to take place, each of the citizens of Samaria (and of the whole of the northern kingdom) will be taken straight out through the holes in the wall and led to Harmon.

Scholars have not been able to identify Harmon, but it obviously is a place of humiliation. Amos 5:27 says that they will be taken 'into exile beyond Damascus'; that is Harmon.

Self-gratifying religion (4:4-5)

These foolish women thought that if warnings about God's judgement coming upon them were true, then they could be averted if they spent a bit more time in religious activities. This is why Amos teases them about these thoughts. He says, 'Go to Bethel …; go to Gilgal … Bring your sacrifices … your tithes … a thank-offering … your freewill offerings'. Both Bethel and Gilgal were notable places in the history of Israel. Bethel was possibly the site where Jacob worshipped God after receiving the promise of Abraham from God (Gen. 28:10-22; 35:1-15); and Gilgal, which was near Jericho, was where Joshua set up the twelve stones taken from the Jordan after the children of Israel crossed over into the Promised Land (Josh. 4:19-20; 5:1-10). Instead of being used to remind the people of God's faithfulness, they had been turned into places of (almost pagan) worship.

As we saw earlier, Jeroboam had set up two altars in Israel, one at Bethel and the other at Dan. He made golden calves and set them up in each place; and told his people, 'Here are your gods, O Israel, who brought you up out of Egypt' (1 Kings 12:28). Scholars are not sure why Gilgal was cited by Amos, but certainly sacrifices had been offered to the Lord on an altar there when Saul was anointed king in that place (1 Sam. 11:15; 13:8-12).

We can see that this 'religious' activity was merely to meet the people's own selfish ends. Earlier in their history offerings were brought only once a year (see 1 Sam. 1:3, 7 and 21). And the tithes, a tenth of a person's income, were usually paid just once a year, or sometimes just every third year. A footnote to 4:4 in the NIV suggests that Amos was calling the people to give 'tithes on the third day'. These sacrifices and tithes were 'over the top'. It seems that they were given more to impress God, and perhaps their fellow citizens, than to show their gratitude and love to the Lord. Some of the other prophets pick up this point. Hosea says that God is more interested in loyalty than sacrifices (Hos. 6:6) and Micah shows that God requires justice, love and humility rather than a thousand rams or ten thousand rivers of oil (Micah 6:6-8).

> The Bible makes it very clear how Christians should live their lives but so often we think we know a better way. We try to convince ourselves that the Scriptures mean something other than what they clearly say; or we think that a particular verse does not apply to us.

The people were used to burning 'leavened bread as a thank-offering' (v. 5). Yet God had made it clear that only unleavened bread was to be offered in sacrifices (Lev. 7:12-13). Furthermore, these were to be offered with humility. They ought not to 'brag' or 'boast' about their sacrifices when they came to worship the Lord. Years later, the Lord Jesus Christ was to urge his people to 'Be careful not to do your "acts of righteousness" before men, to be seen by them' (Matt. 6:1); in fact our giving should be done in secret (Matt. 6:4).

The Bible makes it very clear how Christians should live their lives but so often we think we know a better way. We try to convince ourselves that the Scriptures mean something other than what they clearly say; or we think that a particular verse does not apply to us. Just like the people of Amos's day we assume that we know best and the outcome is that we forget God's Word (see Ps. 119:16).

FOR FURTHER STUDY

1. Read Deuteronomy 32:14; Psalm 22:12; Isaiah 2:13; Jeremiah 50:19; Ezekiel 27:6; Micah 7:14; 39:18. What kind of picture do we get of Bashan?

2. Read Hebrews 6:13,16. How do these verses help us understand what God says about his oath in Amos 6:8 and 8:7?

3. The place of Jacob's blessing had become an altar of meaningless ritual. What was the difference in the worship of God in Genesis 35:1-7 compared with that in Amos 4:4-5 and 5:21-22?

TO THINK ABOUT AND DISCUSS

1. Compare the behaviour of the women in Amos 4:1 with the pattern outlined by Peter in 1 Peter 3:1-6. In our day we have many pressures put upon us to be self-assertive. How can the principles laid down by Peter be worked out in today's equal opportunities society?

2. How do some of the actions of modern Christians offend against God's holiness? (See 1 Thes. 3:13; 2 Tim. 1:9.)

3. In what ways is the Western church of today ignoring God's clear commands?

7 Ignoring God's voice

(4:6-13)

Many Christians and churches are so busy with religious activities that they often neglect the spiritual and physical needs of those around them. In doing so they are ignoring the clear commands of the God they claim to be worshipping.

A mos highlights the same kinds of issues when he chastises the women of the northern kingdom who had been indulging in pleasure instead of caring for the needs of the poor. He also censures their husbands who had been boasting about their religious 'worship' instead of obeying the Lord.

Lessons from history (4:6-11)

'Why doesn't God do something?' people often cry. In this section of Amos the prophet points out five things that God had been doing. Each of these had caused the people a great deal of heartache but, sadly, they failed to realize that God was speaking to them through these disasters. They were so busy with their lives that it did not occur to them to ask why these had come about. So Amos, speaking the words of God, informs them in no uncertain manner: '[It was] I [who] gave you empty stomachs…' (v.6). 'I also withheld rain from you …' (v.7). 'I struck your gardens and vineyards … with blight…' (v.9). 'I sent plagues among you' (v.10); 'I overthrew some of you…' (v.11).

These disasters, then, did not happen by chance, nor were they caused by a foreign power. God had a divine purpose to fulfil through these things. He grieved over the people's selfishness, and he wanted them to repent. But he also knew that even when they feigned sorrow for their sins, they would soon slide back into their old ways. God wanted them to repent wholeheartedly and acknowledge their disobedience to his clear commands. Sadly this chastisement had no effect and we catch a glimpse of the heart of God at the end of each of these sections: '"Yet you have not returned to me," declares the LORD' (vv.6,8,9,10,11).

Therefore the Lord reminded them of some of the things that had happened in their past history. There had been years when they had gone hungry. On other occasions the harvest was poor. This led to further anguish, because it rained in some parts of the land while other areas suffered drought, causing jealousy and the need to stagger from town to town to collect water. At other times they suffered from blight and mildew and swarms of locusts.

Amos paints a vivid picture of their experiences during the many years that followed their deliverance from the bondage of Egypt. They had also been attacked by human enemies resulting in great slaughter. The reminder of the well-known story of the destruction of the cities of the plain—Sodom and Gomorrah—ought to have served as a warning against those who persisted in wickedness. Not even ten righteous people had been found in those cities (Gen. 18:16-33) so God destroyed them, and only righteous Lot (see 2 Peter 2:6-7) and his children were saved. Their deliverance was 'like a burning stick snatched from the fire'.

Surely, cried Amos, the reminder of these and other tragedies must drive the people to throw up their hands in horror and cast themselves upon the Lord? But even these things failed to awaken any response.

Prepare for judgement (4:12-13)

The Lord now sums up the severity of his judgements by saying, 'This is what I will do to you'. The fact that 'this' is not detailed here only serves to highlight the fear of the unknown judgement. Therefore, the people of Israel must 'prepare to meet [their] God.'

We have a similar scene in Exodus 19 when the Lord descended on Mount Sinai in fire. 'Smoke billowed up from it like smoke from a furnace, the whole mountain trembled violently, and the sound of the trumpet grew louder and louder.' Then Moses 'led the people out of the camp to meet with God, and they stood at the foot of the mountain' (Exod. 19:17-19). There the people were to receive the blessings of the law. But in the case of Amos, they were to prepare to meet their God in judgement.

The power and majesty of the Lord are outlined in the last verse of chapter 4. He is not only the creator who forms the mountains, creates the power of the wind and turns dawn into darkness; he is also the one who reveals his thoughts to man and treads the high places of the earth. 'The LORD God Almighty is his name.'

Israel had sinned grievously, and despite many entreaties to repent, they had not done so. They are like Christians today; even the best among us who are reading this book have also broken God's laws and have failed to live lives honouring to him. Therefore, the same judgement awaits each one of us because 'the wages of sin is death' (Rom. 6:23). Every one of us will have to stand before the judgement seat of God (Rom. 14:10 and 2 Cor. 5:10). But through the atoning death of the Lord Jesus Christ on the cross of Calvary, those who truly repent and turn to him in faith will learn that Christ has borne the

> Even the best among us who are reading this book have also broken God's laws and have failed to live lives honouring to him. Therefore, the same judgement awaits each one of us because 'the wages of sin is death' (Rom. 6:23)...Those who truly repent and turn to him in faith will learn that Christ has borne the punishment that was due to them.

punishment that was due to them. Sadly, though, those who refuse to 'be reconciled to God' (2 Cor. 5:20) will not be protected from the wrath of God on that final judgement day (see Rev. 6:15-17).

1. Read Deuteronomy 28. How many warnings of famine are given here? Read Leviticus 26:13-18. What are the disasters that the Lord promised to bring upon his people if they failed to listen to him and carry out his commands?

2. Read Ecclesiastes 3:17; Matthew 5:21-22; 25:31-33; Hebrews 10:26-27; 1 Peter 4:17. What do these verses teach us about the judgement to come?

3. Look up Psalm 65:3; 135:7; Daniel 2:28; Micah 1:3. What do these verses show us about God's majesty and greatness?

4. What can we learn about the need to be prepared from the Parable of the Tenants (Matt. 21:33-46)?

TO THINK ABOUT AND DISCUSS

1. What should our attitude be when severe trouble comes upon us? (See Job 1:21; Hab. 3:17-19; Phil. 4:10-13.)

2. At what point should we no longer forgive those who have harmed us? (Matt. 18:21-22; 2 Peter 3:9; Rom. 2:4.)

3. How can we use the events happening around us to call people to repentance? (Notice the heart-cry of Jesus over Jerusalem in Matt. 23:37-39.)

8 Lamentation and renewed calls to repentance

(5:1-17)

So far, we have seen that certain judgement is coming upon the northern kingdom of Israel, unless the people turn aside from their sin. When we reach chapter 5 we find that things are becoming even more serious. Judgement is now imminent.

God's lament (5:1-3)

Once again, Amos thunders out, 'Hear this word, O house of Israel' (v.1). The previous two chapters had commenced with a similar call (3:1; 4:1). However, there is something more frightening about the urgency and fervour of these opening verses in chapter 5. The house of Israel is being called to hear a lamentation. This wail is not spelling out disasters which will fall upon others; it is a lament for themselves. Israel is spoken about here as though the nation is already dead, and Amos cries out, 'Fallen is Virgin Israel, never to rise again, deserted in her own land, with no one to lift her up' (v.2).

The northern kingdom is described as 'Virgin Israel'. Here the word 'virgin' is not used because she is clean and pure, but because she has been living independently of God and of godly people. She is a virgin in the sense that she is alone. Amos speaks as though Israel is dead and already lying buried in her grave. It is at this point that we see the prophecies of 3:11 and 4:3 coming to fruition. Not only will Israel's allies in the surrounding nations fail to come to her aid, but even her God himself will refuse to come and lift her up out of her lifeless state.

The death of someone who is unrepentant is a terrifying thing to witness. When I am taking funeral services I refuse to read Canon Henry Scott Holland's popular poem which commences, 'Death is nothing at all. I have only slipped away into the next room ...' I will not read this because it is untrue; death is not inconsequential. Death is the wages of sin (Rom. 6:23). Death came into the world as a result of Adam's disobedience. To die 'without hope and without God' (Eph. 2:12) is a horrifying thing.

Amos tells us that the nation of Israel was 'dead and done for'; she would soon be no more. Shortly, she would be carried away and treated abominably—and then extinguished, never to rise again. Sadly some 'churches' today are in that same state of a 'living' death. They continue to go through the motions of holding services and doing good works (in their own name). Like the church at Sardis, they have 'a reputation of being alive' but in fact they are 'dead' (Rev. 3:1).

Even though Amos is reading out God's 'funeral service' over Israel, sadly she will still refuse to be humbled. Instead, with a great show of pride she will act like a 'city that marches out a thousand strong' or 'like a town that marches out a hundred strong'. Even though she has been warned in unmistakable tones, she fails to heed the warning, and the result will be that she will meet an implacable enemy and crawl home completely destroyed. This is not idle talk or speculation, it is 'what the Sovereign LORD says' (v. 3).

God's gracious call to repentance (5:4-6)

The people of Israel had always made much of their religion. They were proud of the fact that they were God's chosen people and they fancied they were doing their religious duties by flocking to the religious places of worship, especially at festival times. This may have impressed the nations around them but God saw through their insincerity. He knew that it was all worthless show.

In these two verses, Amos highlights three places of historical and religious significance—Bethel, Gilgal and Beersheba. In 4:5-6 Amos had already referred to Bethel and Gilgal; now he adds Beersheba to the list. Although these were popular places of worship which grew crowds of 'worshippers', sadly the people were merely 'going through the motions' of faith. One vital element was missing. They were not seeking the Lord.

The consequence of these serious failures was clear to Amos. He told them, 'The LORD will sweep through the house of Joseph like a fire; it will devour [and no one will be able to] quench [its destructive force]'. They, the northern

> In the midst of this talk about destruction it is amazing that God still urges the people to seek his grace and mercy, just as the Lord encouraged the church at Sardis to turn to him (Rev. 3:2-3). All he requires of his people is that they will come to him, and they will live, and not die.

kingdom, will never 'rise again' (v.2) because God's destroying fire will burn them up.

In the midst of this talk about destruction it is amazing that God still urges the people to seek his grace and mercy, just as the Lord encouraged the church at Sardis to turn to him (Rev. 3:2-3). All he requires of his people is that they will come to him, and they will live, and not die. Later in their history, Ezekiel would cry out to the people of God, 'Why will you die? ... I take no pleasure in the death of anyone, declares the Sovereign LORD'. Because of this, God called them to 'Repent and live!' (Ezek. 18:31-32). The Lord Jesus Christ himself, even while he was denouncing the city of Jerusalem cried out, 'O Jerusalem, Jerusalem ... how often I have longed to gather your children together, as a hen gathers her chicks under her wings'. Then his heart-cry went out, 'but you were not willing' (Matt. 23:37-38).

Like Naaman (in 2 Kings 5:13), the people of Israel were not being called upon to do some great thing, even though they would probably have a strong desire and willingness to do something that would help to make them feel worthy of

God's mercy. All that the Lord asked of them was simply to 'seek me and live' (v.4) but despite his gracious invitation, they refused and would not do so.

People are the same today. Many go to great lengths to try to gain God's attention. On the Greek island of Tinos I have seen women crawling on their knees all the way from the lower part of the main town to the large Roman Catholic church at the top of the hill. They do this because they are barren and are seeking God's gift of a child, or to receive some other blessing. In other places, individuals put themselves through great anguish in fasting for many days, recite lengthy prayers, or attend hours of religious services. They will do these arduous acts, yet they neglect the simple gospel message to 'seek me and live' (v.4). The Lord Jesus Christ makes it clear that all God requires is for people to humble themselves and come to him and find rest (Matt. 11:28).

In the midst of all their religious observances, God tells them that he will 'sweep through the house of Joseph like a fire; it will devour, and Bethel will have no one to quench it' (v.6). Fire is a very destructive force which quickly spreads and devours all in its path, yet another picture of the imminent judgement of God upon the people. Amos had used the same picture earlier (1:7,10,1214; 2:2,5) but here 'God himself is pictured as a devouring fire that destroys everything (cf. 7:4-6)'.[14]

God's power displayed (5:7-13)

From his denunciations against Israel at the end of verse 6, Amos now gives startling evidence of the people's failure to obey God's laws. The Lord addresses them personally, and shouts at them, 'You who turn justice into bitterness and cast righteousness to the ground …' (v.7). But before he continues with the list of their sins he focuses their eyes on himself. To contrast what the people do (in turning justice into bitterness), the Lord now shows what he does. He also reminds them that he changes things, and these activities demonstrate real power—the power of the Almighty.

The words of verses 8 and 9 are a kind of hymn which interrupts the catalogue of Israel's sins (which are again reflected in v.10). The message is clear: there is a tremendous contrast between what man changes, and what God changes. What the Lord does is not turn justice into bitterness, but night into day, and day into night (v.8). He created the earth and sky out of nothing.

Amos illustrates God's creation by referring to the Pleiades (a group of seven easily visible stars—in fact there are many more in this group) and Orion ('the hunter', lying very near the Pleiades in the northern sky). Whatever strength men may believe they have, their power is as nothing in comparison to the might of the Lord who 'makes', 'turns', 'calls', 'pours' (v.8) 'flashes destruction' and 'brings … to ruin' (v.9).

In verse 10 Amos returns to some of the activities of the people of Israel. He continues to address them in personal tones: 'You hate the one who reproves in court and despises him who tells the truth'. Although they had been to Bethel to worship, they are totally unaltered. Rather than seeking righteousness and justice for all, they are solely concerned for their own selfish ends. Once again it is the poor who suffer.

They are trampled upon and forced to part with their hard-earned grain. The wealthy people of the land had built stone mansions for themselves and planted lush vineyards but the fact is they would not reap the benefit of these material things. The enormity of sin might be concealed from man, but God knows how many are our offences, and how great are our sins.

The prudent man, although deprived of justice, is wise because he does not complain 'in such times'. He keeps silent because he knows 'the days are evil' (v.13). But he knows too, that unlike the wealthy people of Israel, God is just and one day he will vindicate the innocent and they will be honoured because of their righteousness.

Seek God, or else…! (5:14-17)

At first sight verses 14 and 15 appear to be similar to verses 4 and 5, but when we look more closely we see that there is a distinct change of emphasis. In the earlier passage the theme is about seeking God in worship instead of merely wanting to be in a 'religious place'. Here the driving force is the necessity of right living. Amos now addresses 'the remnant of Joseph', those who are the faithful ones of Israel. They are called 'the remnant of Joseph' because they have demonstrated a moral transformation in their lives. 'The remnant [motif] of Amos is not based on some ancient promise, but is a matter of the grace of God'.[15]

The people are to 'seek good, not evil'. The evil referred to

> The enormity of sin might be concealed from man, but God knows how many are our offences, and how great are our sins.

is that of depriving the poor of their food (v.11) and of justice (vv.12,7). They are also to 'hate evil [and] love good' (v.15).

If they behave in this way (because they have a living faith in the living God—v.6), they will experience the presence of the Lord God Almighty, just as he promised to be with them. If they 'maintain justice in the courts' then 'perhaps the LORD God Almighty will have mercy on the remnant of Joseph' (v.15). He says 'perhaps' to emphasize that God's mercy is not something that can be earned or merited in any way. It is purely of God's sovereign will that his grace is imparted to repentant sinners.

> In these two verses the call to repentance now has an ethical nature to it. 'There is to be an earnest longing for good and rejection of evil in the heart matched by practical godly living'.

In these two verses the call to repentance now has an ethical nature to it. 'There is to be an earnest longing for good and rejection of evil in the heart matched by practical godly living'.[16] The demand for a change of mind and heart is just as strong here as it was later in Paul's sermon delivered on the Areopagus: '[God] commands all people everywhere to repent' (Acts 17:30). But we must remember that 'Men are forgiven when they repent, not because they repent'.[17]

In verses 16 and 17 we return to the theme of the destruction of Israel. Because of their sin and their refusal to repent, great wailing will come all over the land. This is not Amos's assessment; it is what 'the Lord, the LORD God

Almighty, says.' In these two verses there are numerous mentions of 'wailing', 'anguish' and of 'mourners'.

All of the people, in every place, will be taken up with the overwhelming sadness and pain that is coming upon them from their enemies. This time the Lord will not pass over them, as he did at the time of the Exodus (see Exod. 12:13,23). On this coming day of judgement the Lord will do to Israel as he did to the Egyptians long before: he will pass through their midst and bring destruction upon them (see 3:11).

For further study ▶

FOR FURTHER STUDY

1. The 'remnant of Joseph' refers to the northern kingdom of Israel. This is sometimes called Ephraim because Ephraim was the leading tribe in the kingdom of Israel. Read Genesis 39:2,21,23 and 41:38. In what ways was the Lord with Joseph?

2. Read James 2:14-26. What is the relationship between faith and good works, according to this passage?

TO THINK ABOUT AND DISCUSS

1. What are the 'marks of death' in a church (see 2 Peter 2 and Jude 5-19)? What are the essential beliefs and practices that a spiritually alive church, or group of churches, must have (see Acts 2:37-47)?

2. What do you say to a friend who says to you, 'I go to church at Christmas and Easter; isn't that enough to please God?'? (See the comments on 5:4-5 and also 4:4-5.)

3. What guidance would you give to someone who is seeking to please God solely through religious ceremonial?

4. Can a person be born again if he or she does not give any evidence of a life changed for the better? (See Gal. 5:6; 1 Thes. 1:3; 2 Thes. 1:11; James 2:22.)

9 Seeking escape by hope which is false

(5:18-27)

When I am visiting an unbelieving family after the death of a loved one, quite often someone says, 'He/she's in a better place now'. Such a person does not understand that the Bible clearly teaches that death is not an escape from judgement. Instead it is either an entrance into a glorious life with Christ, or it is the beginning of everlasting punishment.

The day of the Lord (5:18-20)

The people of Israel were longing for the coming of the day of the Lord, because they assumed that this would usher in a time of victory over their enemies. This is why they regularly went to the sacred places and offered sacrifices. They assumed that this would guarantee peace and contentment.

Yet Amos had constantly been telling them all was not well between them and God; they needed to repent and seek his mercy, but their pride had got in the way of repentance. So, in verses 18-27 we see that what they expected to be deliverance would, in fact, turn out to be the beginning of their deportation and destruction. In other words the 'day of the LORD' would not bring for them a time of glorious light; it would bring them into the darkness of death (see 5:1-2).

> The day of the Lord, for unrepentant sinners, will not be a time when the sun is shining a ray of hope upon them. Instead there will be darkness—pitch-darkness, without one tiny ray of hope.

The prophet vividly describes what it will be like for those who try to escape from God's wrath rather than 'seek [him] and live' (v.4). They will have the same kind of fleeting relief that people might have if they escape from the clutches of a lion only to discover they have run straight into the path of a fierce bear. Then, should they manage to move fast enough to reach the safety of their home and slam the door shut behind them, they would find danger inside. Furthermore, in the process of leaning against their wall, to get their breath back, they would come into contact with poisonous snakes which would bite them and cause poisonous venom to flow quickly through their veins.

So, the day of the Lord, for unrepentant sinners, will not be a time when the sun is shining a ray of hope upon them. Instead there will be darkness—pitch-darkness, without one tiny ray of hope.

Here we see the folly of attempting to run away from God;

they will not succeed because the Lord is hard on their heels. Amos wrote his message a long time ago but his words have great relevance for today. They tell us that those who die unsaved will one day come face to face with their sin (even if they assumed they had lived a respectable life). The good news for us, as it was for the people in the days of Amos, is that the Lord is still calling out, 'Seek me and live'. Those who heed his gracious invitation will gladly fall into his arms and be saved, but those who refuse will be destroyed (2 Peter 2:7).

But there is meaning here also for true believers in the Lord Jesus Christ. None of us is immune from the desire to run away from the demands that the Lord makes upon us. We will not be able to avoid the cost of discipleship for ever. One day we will have to say 'none of self and all of thee'.[18] He requires of all who love him complete obedience to his commands (see John 14:23).

The folly of mere 'religion' (5:21-27)

This section starts with severe words (vv.21-23). Regarding the 'religion' of the majority of the Israelites, God says, 'I hate, I despise … I cannot stand …I will not accept … I will have no regard … I will not listen.' Isaiah said the same kind of thing to those of the southern kingdom. 'I have more than enough of burnt offerings … I have no pleasure in the blood of bulls and lambs and goats' (Isa. 1:11).

Notice that the Lord is not saying that these offerings in themselves are wrong; it is the condition of the people's hearts, and their disregard for the welfare of the people, that is sinful. They thought they were obeying God's laws but they were performing these ceremonies through habit—and out of an unloving sense of duty. Their songs of praise came from impure hearts.

Then in verse 24, we turn to the positive side of Amos's message. He calls upon the people to 'Let justice roll on like a river, righteousness like a never-failing stream!' It is as though they had been keeping their worship locked up in formal ritual, but God wanted their enjoyment of him to burst out in blessed acclamation. He did not want their acts of justice and righteousness merely to trickle out of them, but wanted them to rush out, like a noisy torrent down the mountains—and his desire was that the people should be free from the dirt and filth of sin. Furthermore, he looked for these things to continue. Their acts of love and fairness were to cascade like a 'never-failing stream.'

No longer does God speak about drought. Amos relates this water to justice and righteousness. Like rivers or streams, the Israelites should not keep the benefit of their worship to themselves. Instead, the blessings of God ought to gush out from them, having a good effect on the people living around them. Jesus tells us that we should 'let [our] light shine before men, that they may see [our] good deeds and praise [not us, but our] Father in heaven' (Matt. 5:16).

However, this was not yet happening. The people had been carrying out their religious feasts and had entered into the externals of worship. Neither justice nor righteousness was flowing out to others because the hearts of the people were not right before God, and they were proud of their efforts. Burnt offerings and grain offerings are mentioned, but there is no reference to any sin offering. Perhaps the people were not aware that they were sinful and needed to experience God's forgiveness. There was no point in their offering these other sacrifices if they were not totally consecrated to God, and they failed to look upwards to the Lord and outwards to other people.

If they had looked into their history—when they had brought 'sacrifices and offerings for forty years in the desert'—they would have discovered that these offerings were not enough. Perhaps in an effort to pacify their potential invader (Assyria) they had incorporated some of the Assyrian gods into their worship (v.26). In verses 25 and 26, 'Amos is contrasting the true religion of the nation in the wilderness with the false worship of his day'.[19] These gods (Sakkuth and Kaiwan—NIV footnotes) refer to Saturn, the supreme light in the sky after the sun and the moon. So now they were not only failing to worship the Lord with purity of heart, they were also incorporating false gods into their adoration.

The outcome of all this would be that God would send them into exile, 'beyond Damascus'—i.e. into Assyria.

For further study ▶

FOR FURTHER STUDY

1. Read Matthew 25:1-13. What does this parable teach us about the 'day of the Lord'?

2. Read these verses on 'the end of the wicked' in Matthew: 5:22; 10:28; 18:9; 23:15; 23:33. Notice that Jesus spoke more about the eternal destruction of hell than did any other person. Compare these verses with the statements in James 3:6, 2 Peter 2:4 and Revelation 6:12-17.

3. What are some of the implications of being a disciple of Christ? (See Matt. 19:27; Luke 14:25-34; John 12:25-26.)

TO THINK ABOUT AND DISCUSS

1. What is your heart like when you go to a church service? Do you just enjoy the rhythm and melody of the songs you sing in church, or do you really enter into the heart of worship? Does the beat of the band's percussion make a bigger impact upon you than the words that you sing? Compare your feelings with what the Lord requires in regard to justice and righteousness in Hosea 6:6; Micah 6:8; John 4:23-24; Ephesians 4:24; 5:19.

2. What will the 'day of the Lord' mean for believers, and for those who have no faith in Christ? (See Matt. 25:1-13; Rom. 2:6-10; 1 Cor. 6:19-20; 2 Cor. 5:10.) What are the implications of this for how we live our lives?

3. How can we avoid incorporating false gods into Christian worship? How do success, affluence and materialism contaminate our worship of God? (See Ps. 24:3-5; 2 Cor. 6:14-18; James 1:27.)

10 The dangers of man-made security

(6:1-14)

When we wake up to a morning that is bright and sunny after a good night's sleep, it is natural to feel a sense of wellbeing. It does us little harm occasionally to experience moments like these. It is good to feel that we have done our best and can now look forward to a period of peace and hope. However, this can be a dangerous position. None of us should be so elated by our achievements that we think we can 'rest on our laurels'.

The complacency of Israel (6:1-7).

The people of Israel appear to have taken little notice of the demands made by Amos. Perhaps they had felt quite smug when they heard the prophet condemning the selfishness of their women (see 4:1). They may have suffered no disquiet when the Lord's servant uttered his 'woes' against those of a more religious frame of mind—those who had been longing for the day of the Lord to arrive (5:18). Little did these men realize that it was now their turn to come under the prophet's searching eye (that is, under God's gaze). At the beginning of Amos 6, the prophet shattered their false sense of security. His voice seemed to rise to an even great volume than before as he called out to them, 'Woe to you who are complacent in Zion'.

He is addressing the 'notable men of the foremost nation'. In other words, it was the leaders of the people of Israel who were subject to these 'woes'. However, it was not just the northern Israelites who were spoken to; he called out to all those 'who feel secure on Mount Samaria'—i.e. Judah as well. These people of the southern kingdom may have forgotten their brief mention in 2:4-5, but now they are included in the condemnation because in God's eyes Israel actually was made up of all twelve tribes.

> They were like those who do not want to think about the future days, especially their forthcoming deaths. Such people just want to live for today; they do not want to think about tomorrow and what it might bring.

Amos challenged all of these men (from both kingdoms) to look around them. He called attention to their pride (see also 6:8) and their boasting over the capture of the cities of Calneh and Hamath (to the north). These had been incorporated into the northern part of Israel (perhaps during the campaign of Jeroboam II—see 2 Kings 14:28) just as Gath had been included into the southern kingdom in the days of Uzziah (2 Chr. 26:6).

The Lord asked them whether these other cities were better off than their own two kingdoms. He also enquired, 'Was their land larger than yours?' They would have immediately thought to themselves, 'No. These others were not better off, nor did their land occupy more space than ours'.

In view of that, was it not surprising that the rulers of these other cities were behaving much more sensibly than the people of God? Unlike Israel, they were far from complacent because they were well aware of the danger facing them and were taking active means to defend themselves against the invader.

The prophet then hammers his message home by roaring out, 'You put off the evil day' (v.5). He meant that they were like those who do not want to think about the future days, especially their forthcoming deaths. Such people just want to live for today; they do not want to think about tomorrow and what it might bring.

If we ignore our responsibilities and think that by doing so 'the evil day' will be pushed further and further into the future, then we are in for an unpleasant surprise. By acting like this we are, in effect, bringing nearer the judgement day. If our sole occupation is our present enjoyment then we are ignoring this fact: time is marching onwards.

When I was a boy a popular song said,

Enjoy yourself. It's later than you think!

Enjoy yourself. While you're still in the pink!

The years go by, as quickly as a wink.

Enjoy yourself. Enjoy yourself.

It's later than you think.[20]

In a sense, that song speaks the truth. If we think only of 'today', we will actually discover that the future arrives very quickly. For the vast majority of the people of Israel, the days ahead of them were going to be 'a reign of terror' (see 5:27 and 6:7). So even though the judgement was drawing near, the people were 'putting off the evil day' by lazing around and enjoying the passing luxuries of the present.

In verses 4-6 Amos paints a decadent picture of their shame. Their relaxation was not the outcome of some wonderful and pleasing activity. They had nothing to boast about, apart from their wealth. Amos condemns them because they were luxuriating in a selfish lifestyle, while all around them the poor were in great need.

Throughout history, there have been rich people who have enjoyed a sumptuous standard of living without giving a thought to the sufferings of others. It seems incredible that in the awful Auschwitz concentration camp of the Second World War, Nazi officers could enjoy wonderful banquets, even calling on some of the Jews to play music to them before they were taken to the gas chambers. The 'notable men' of Israel lolled on beds of ivory in drunken stupors, eating choice lambs and fattened calves, and singing drunken songs—accompanied by music that was a travesty of the style of the great King David (5:23; see 1 Sam. 16:15-23 and 2 Sam. 23:1). Their whole lifestyle was a mockery of all that was honest, good and true. They covered themselves in expensive perfumed ointments, thinking that they would hide the stench of their foul breath and atrocious behaviour.

All this was done by those who thought of themselves as leaders of the people—yet they did not shed one tear over the 'ruin of Joseph'—Israel's wretched condition. This phrase reminds us of the patriarch Joseph, whose brothers cast him into a deep, foul pit, caring little for his distress. Even Reuben, who wanted to rescue Joseph, did nothing (Gen. 37:23-25 and 42:21).

Amos makes it clear that these 'notable men' of Israel demanded preferential treatment and recognition. And that is exactly what they got. God promised that they would be the first—but the first to be dragged off as captives (6:7). In fact he declared that they would be 'at the head of the defeat march into captivity'.[21] Now, instead of drunken revelry, they would discover that the party was over and the end had come.

The pride of Israel (6:8-14)

Now there is a solemn declaration of God's word. 'The Sovereign LORD has sworn by himself—the LORD God Almighty declares'. In Genesis 22:1-18, Abraham demonstrated his allegiance to God and his faithfulness to his word by being prepared to offer up his only, well-loved son as a sacrifice to God. Because he did this, the angel of the Lord told him that God had sworn by himself that he would surely bless Abraham and grant him many descendants. God swore by himself because there is no greater one than he (see Heb. 6:13). Twice the name of the 'LORD' is mentioned in verse 8, to show that he is declaring his final verdict upon disobedient Israel.

In no uncertain terms the root of Israel's problem is stated as 'pride'. The Lord abhors the pride of Jacob. By using the name of Jacob he is reminding the people that Jacob had twelve sons; therefore this stinging rebuke is addressed to the whole of Israel—all twelve tribes. God was not impressed by their puny fortresses, which they had assumed would protect them from their enemies. He was going to 'deliver up' the whole of the city, i.e. the people of God, and everything they had.

Down through the ages God's people have been eaten up with pride. The people of Edom were proud of their lofty city (see Obadiah). Not only does pride go before a fall (Prov. 16:18) but God tells us that he opposes the proud and gives grace to the humble (1 Peter 5:5). The godliest people have been characterized by humility. If we have achieved anything of any real worth, then it is because the Lord has been working through us. Not only did the Lord detest the pride of Jacob then, but he still takes no pleasure in a proud person. Jesus taught that 'Whoever exalts himself will be humbled' (Matt. 23:12). His desire is that we humble ourselves under his mighty hand (James 4:6 and 1 Peter 5:6).

> Down through the ages God's people have been eaten up with pride.

In verses 9 and 10 the prophet gives an example of the kind of complete destruction that will come upon the people. He imagines a house where ten men are cowering. Bluntly he declares, 'They too will die'. Later a relative arrives to deal with the dead by cremating them, illustrating the complete removal of Israel. The relative asks a neighbour, 'Is anyone with you?' and he tells him there is no one left in the house. As this is a very solemn moment, the Lord's name must not pass anyone's lips. Everyone must be silent before the Lord (see Hab. 2:20; Zeph. 1:7 and Zech. 2:13).

Because the Lord has given the orders, no one will escape the judgement. Not only will all types of people be deported, but even their houses will be demolished, whether they are the great houses which were the pride of the wealthy, or the small houses of the poor. God will demolish the pride of both rich and poor.

Amos draws attention to the absurdity of the situation by asking two seemingly foolish questions. 'Do horses run on the rocky crags? Does one plough there with oxen?' Of course, no one would dream of making horses work on jagged rocky outcrops; the level field was the normal place of activity. Yet, by their actions, God's people were completely reversing the normal way of working. Instead of justice being a precious, longed-for commodity, by their selfish, uncaring actions they had turned it into poison. Not only was Israel's justice unfair, it was deadly. Instead of them producing wonderful fruits of righteousness, all that they achieved was bitterness.

The prophet piles on the irony even more strongly; these arrogant people did not give God the glory when they achieved military victories. Sarcastically, Amos points out that they rejoiced in the conquest of Lo Debar, saying, 'Did we not take Karnaim by our own strength?' (v.13). The significance of these towns lies in their names. Lo Debar means 'nothing' and Karnaim means 'horns'. Perhaps Amos was pointing out that their 'strength had been for nothing'.[22]

Verse 14 commences in the same way as verse 11—'The LORD God Almighty declares'. This verses emphasizes again the certainty of God's action. God has already chosen another nation to be victorious over Israel. The compass of the land is described by saying that this destruction will occur 'all the way from Lebo Hamath [in the north] to the valley of the Arabah [thought to be the Dead Sea].' God's servant would descend upon them, oppress them and take them out of their land for ever.

Israel had not taken God seriously, nor heeded the many warnings given by the prophets. Their pride in what they considered to be their own achievements, the refusal to practise righteousness and justice, and their growing apostasy led to their downfall. The Lord was going to demonstrate that he means what he says, and he would carry out his will.

Proverbs 14:34 declares that 'Righteousness exalts a nation, but sin is a disgrace to any people'. This is still true and sadly many nations are behaving as though they are the masters of their own destiny. Blessed is the nation whose God is the Lord (Ps. 33:12), but woe to the nation whose pride prevents its people from obeying God's Word.

FOR FURTHER STUDY

1. Read the Parable of the Rich Fool in Luke 12:16-21. How did this man show his complacency? What does the Bible say about laziness and its dangers? (See Prov. 6:9-10; 24:33-34; Isa. 56:12; Ezek. 34:2-3.)

2. Notice that it is the things that come out of the mouth which make a person 'unclean' (Mark 7:20-23). In the AV the word 'arrogance' (NIV) is translated 'pride'. How is pride related to all the other evil desires in these verses?

TO THINK ABOUT AND DISCUSS

1. How can we avoid becoming complacent in our Christian lives? (See Isa. 32:9-11; Luke 6:24-26; John 9:4; Rom. 13:11-14; Eph. 5:14-16.)

2. What can we learn from Israel's experiences in these opening verses of Amos 6 and how can we seek to remedy these faults? (See 2 Cor. 6:14-18; 1 Tim. 3:1-6; Heb. 13:7,17; James 4:7-10.)

3. Israel had drifted away from the Lord and his ways. When things go wrong in our personal lives, and the life of our churches, what action should be taken? (See Matt. 18:15-20; 1 Cor. 5:1-13; James 5:13-16; 1 John 5:16.)

4. To what extent should we take pleasure in a job which we have done well? How can we prevent such pleasure from becoming pride? (See Matt. 23:12; James 4:6; 1 Peter 5:6; 1 John 2:15-17.)

11 God's judgements illustrated and Amos's response

(7:1-9)

This chapter commences the final third of the prophecy. In these closing scenes we discover that God gives Amos five visions (in 7:1—9:10) and five promises (in 9:11-15). Here we look at the first three of these five visions

The locusts and the fire (7:1-6)

God rams home his message by illustrating the effect of his judgements on the disobedient people of Israel. These visions are not set in mystifying language but are clear and plain for everyone to grasp. Verses 1 and 4 of chapter 7 and verse 1 of chapter 8 all commence with these words, 'This is what the Sovereign Lord showed me'. God is reminding Amos and the people that these visions are of great importance.

The first thing that he saw was the Lord preparing swarms

of locusts (v.1). These small insects can devastate whole crops within a few minutes. Amos also saw the crop beginning to sprout again after the king's animals had already eaten the first green shoots (maybe as payment for the royal tax). However, when this second, stronger growth of crops was just coming into view, the prophet saw the swarms of locusts chomping their way through every field until the whole land had been 'stripped clean'. This was a dreadful thing to happen, particularly for people who depended upon agriculture for the majority of their food. This would mean severe shortages of food for everyone—except, perhaps, for the royal household.

Amos was distraught when he saw this vision. He did not respond by saying, 'The people deserve this kind of thing because of their disobedience to the Lord's commands.' Instead, his heart went out to the people and he immediately cried out, 'Sovereign Lord, forgive!'

When someone seeks forgiveness they are admitting that they have done wrong. Amos, therefore, does not plead for God to overlook the people's sin. Realizing the danger the people were in, Amos cried out even more, 'How can Jacob survive? He is so small!' Amos is more realistic than the 'notable men' who felt themselves to be in the 'foremost nation' of Israel (see 6:1). Although they were big in their own eyes, they were puny in God's sight. This is why Amos pleaded earnestly for the Lord to forgive them.

We can learn a great deal by observing the tenderness of Amos's heart as he pleads with God for them (vv.2b, 5a). We all live among people who have disobeyed God's laws and we know that, without turning to Christ for forgiveness, everyone is doomed. But do we have a similar love for our neighbours as Amos had for Israel? Certainly like Ezekiel, we should warn them of the danger they are in (Ezek. 3:18-19) but should we not also copy Amos's actions? We should urge them to 'pursue God's pardon as we would pursue anything of surpassing value'.[23] Just like Amos, we ought to pour out our hearts in fervent prayer for their salvation because 'the prayer of a righteous man is powerful and effective' (James 5:16). Verses 3 tells us very plainly, 'So the LORD relented.' This means that the numerous swarms of locusts did not descend upon the land. However, the Lord did not promise forgiveness.

The second picture that Amos saw was a great fire that would dry up the great deep and devour the land (v.4). This punishment would be even more overwhelming than the locusts, because now the water under the earth (from which the roots of the crops would draw much of their nourishment) would be dried up in the fierce heat of the fire. Again Amos appeals for his people but this time he is even more intense as he pleads, 'Sovereign LORD, I beg you, stop!' Then he adds as before, 'How can Jacob survive? He is so small.'

When our loved ones, especially our children, are very ill, we immediately pour out our hearts to God, pleading that he will heal and restore them to full health and strength again. This is natural, but do we do the same thing because of the actions of the sinful men and women around us? We are more likely to pray that they will stop being a nuisance.

In answer to Amos's prayer, the Lord did relent and added, 'This will not happen either.' This time (unlike in v. 3) God is described as 'the Sovereign LORD'. God did not relent because Amos forced him to change his mind; rather, the Lord knew from the beginning what he would do. However, we can only see things from a human point of view. As Ray Beeley puts it, God did not change his mind but 'he changed his course of action. He withheld the fully deserved punishment.'24

The plumb-line (7:7-9)

A plumb-line is used to measure the uprightness of walls. Amos knew what a plumb-line was for, and he would certainly have known the purpose of walls—to keep out the enemy. So there was no ambiguity in this vision. When the Lord asked him what he saw, he replied immediately, 'A plumb-line'. It was obvious from the Lord's next statement what he meant; he had set a clear standard for God's people—the law which he had given to them all those years ago at Sinai. Because of their false worship and unjust behaviour they were 'out of true'; they had not been building their lives, and the life of their nation, in strict accordance with God's Word. This had been the repeated message of Amos right from the beginning; the people had deviated from the straight and narrow of God's law, and now they were going to have to suffer for it.

> A plumb-line is used to measure the uprightness of walls. Amos knew what a plumb-line was for, and he would certainly have known the purpose of walls—to keep out the enemy.

Amazingly, in giving this illustration of their sinful behaviour, God calls Israel 'my people'. This is the first time in the book of Amos that God calls them this, but even so he says that he will spare them no longer. He was to tell the people of Judah that, after they had been taken into the captivity of Babylon, he would gather them in his arms and bring them back to their land (Isa. 56:8). But the people of Israel would be spared no longer.

The Lord was also going to destroy 'the high places of Isaac'. It would seem that they had erected various shrines in places associated with their forefathers, as though they thought that this would give them a special sense of holiness, for example at Beersheba where Isaac had worshipped God (Gen. 26:25). But now these areas would be ruined. The people were not to rely on the faith of their fathers; they were to put their trust in God for themselves.

So far the warnings of punishment had been addressed particularly to the 'notable men' of the land (6:1), but now the king and his house are singled out (v.9). God was going to raise his sword of judgement against the whole of Jeroboam's house. This prophecy was fulfilled in about 746B.C. with the assassination of Jeroboam II's son Zechariah (2 Kings 15:10).

FOR FURTHER STUDY

1. Compare the appeal Amos makes on behalf of his people (7:2b and 5a) with the agony God experiences in Hosea 11:8-9.

2. How many times in Amos does God call Israel 'my people' after 7:8, even though he said that he would spare them no longer?

3. In what sense did the Lord 'relent' in 7:3,6? Does the Lord change his mind? Read Ezekiel 18:21-23, 32; 1 Tim. 2:4; 2 Peter 3:9. How can we explain these verses?

TO THINK ABOUT AND DISCUSS

1. Note the urgency of prayers of supplication that we find in the Bible (see Exod. 32:33; 1 Sam. 19:4; 1 Sam. 25:24; Jer. 38:9; Philem. 10). How should we pray for those who are straying from God's paths?

2. We read that 'he who loves [his son] is careful to discipline him' and not 'spare the rod' in Proverbs 13:24, and the writer to the Hebrews tells us that 'the Lord disciplines those he loves' (Heb. 12:6). God often deals with his people in this way in order to bring them to their senses. How have you experienced God's discipline personally, in your church, or in your country?

3. How can we seek to grow in Christian maturity? (See Eph. 4:12-13; Phil. 3:12-16; Col. 4:12; Heb. 5:13-14; James 1:2-6a.)

12 An uncomfortable confrontation

(7:10-17)

It seems that the vision of the plumb-line was the final straw for at least one man—a very important person in this kingdom of Israel.

It was not the king who spoke in verse 10, nor was it one of the noble lords of the land. It was a religious leader. The strong implication is that this man, Amaziah (whose name means 'The Lord is mighty'), was the senior priest in charge of the temple at Bethel. In effect he was 'the archbishop' of this sanctuary (v.13).

In these verses we have an interlude which is very instructive, particularly for those who desire to serve the Lord with wholehearted devotion. Amaziah did not approach Amos; instead he sent a message to Jeroboam, king of Israel. He pointed out that there was a very real enemy at large, not on their borders, but right in the heart of their land. He summed up what Amos had been saying in two phrases—'Amos is raising a conspiracy against you' and 'the land cannot bear all his words' (v.10).

The first of these reports may well have had some truth in

it—except that Amos had not organized a plot to overthrow the government—but the second statement is plain conjecture on the part of Amaziah. Just like all false witnesses, this priest twisted the words of Amos to make his point. He changed Amos's observation that God would rise against the 'house of Jeroboam' (v.9) into a direct attack on the person of Jeroboam II. In fact, history tells us that this king was destined to die naturally (2 Kings 14:29) and not 'by the sword' as Amaziah asserted (v.11). The priest then continued, 'And Israel will surely go into exile, away from their native land'. It is true that Amos had been saying this, but it is strange that the priest did not also mention the prophecy about the destruction of the religious places, especially as he was the priest of Bethel. Perhaps he wanted 'Amos to appear like a political threat and not just a diverse theological opinion that the king might be willing to tolerate'.[25]

Those who wish to attack God's servants and the work of the gospel invariably twist the truth. Sometimes their deviation from fact is only small but they use persuasive words to achieve their evil work. With the authority of an archbishop Amaziah next spoke directly to Amos and said, 'Get out, you seer!' Instead of seeking to have Amos arrested, he urged Amos to leave Israel and return to his homeland, Judah. He told him what he should do (go home) and what he should not do (prophesy at Bethel).

So many people want to deal with difficulties in a similar way. Instead of confronting an issue and putting matters right, their desire is to try to sweep their problems 'under the carpet' to try to avoid any upheaval, or questions. This is not the scriptural way. Although we are required to 'live at peace with everyone' as far as possible (Rom. 12:18), that does not mean that matters of contention should be left unresolved.

We can see from these verses, then, that Amaziah was a coward. He probably knew that Amos was correct in his allegations but instead of siding with him, the priest took the easy way out by insulting him and ordering him to leave the land. In calling him a 'seer' and telling him to 'earn [his] bread' in Judah, Amaziah suggested that Amos was merely 'in it for the money'. In effect he is saying, 'You don't belong here, go back to your own land and enjoy the praise of your own people. We don't want you telling us what to do and what not to do.' And the reason he gave for Amos to leave Bethel was because it was 'the king's sanctuary and the temple of the kingdom' (v.13); Amaziah has been so corrupted by his important position that he does not even pretend that Bethel is God's temple.

Amos's response

Amos did not hesitate to respond to the demand that he should leave the land. He did not try to justify his position, but rather was quick to explain that he 'was neither a prophet nor a prophet's son' (v.14). He never claimed to be a 'professional' prophet; he was one whom the Lord 'took' and commanded to 'prophesy to my people Israel.' (v.15).

He was not ashamed to be a mere shepherd or herdsman who also took care of the sycamore-fig trees. He did not make his living by being a 'professional prophet'. His 'call' to be a prophet did not rest on being trained at one of the schools of the prophets—being one of 'the sons of the prophets'. It depended solely on the fact that God 'took'. He was not ashamed that he did not have the equivalent of a theological university degree.

In answer to Amaziah's charge, Amos replied, 'Now then, hear the word of the LORD. You say, "Do not prophesy against Israel, and stop preaching against the house of Isaac"'. The contrast was between what Amaziah said, and what the Lord had said. Amos, although not a professional prophet, was bold enough to put the high priest of the Bethel sanctuary right by saying, 'I am going to give to you not my words, but "the word of the Lord"'.

This message was very blunt. It was no longer a general call to all of Israel but a specific statement about the future of Amaziah and his family. The Lord's word would be fulfilled and Israel 'will certainly go into exile, away from

> These words highlight the folly of knowing what God is saying but failing to obey it. Amaziah had heard the word of the Lord but rejected it because it did not fit in with his own views or ideas.

their native land' (v.17). The consequence of this would be that Amaziah would also be taken away and 'die in a pagan country', but it seems that his wife and children would remain in Israel. The 'land will be measured and divided up' (including Amaziah's private estate), and the only way in which Amaziah's wife would be able to survive would be to 'become a prostitute in the city'; his children would 'fall by the sword'.

These are terrible things to befall anyone, but these words highlight the folly of knowing what God is saying but failing to obey it. Amaziah had heard the word of the Lord but rejected it because it did not fit in with his own views or ideas. Also, he despised God's servant because he was not a 'professional' clergyman. As high priest of one of the sanctuaries in Israel, he had the responsibility of urging the people to obey the word of the Lord, but he failed in this. Like King Saul he 'rejected the word of the Lord' so he himself was rejected as a servant of God (see 1 Sam. 15:23).

No one should shut their ears to God's word. This is clearly given to us in the Bible and it requires our obedience. It is not only kings and priests (or church leaders) who will have to answer for their disobedience; every one of us will come before the judgement seat of Christ (see 2 Cor. 5:10).

1. Read Job 5:7; Matt. 5:12; John 15:18-21; 2 Cor. 1:3-7; 1 Thes. 3:4; 1 Peter 4:12-19. What do these verses teach us about the testing of faith in the Christian's life?

2. What do we learn about the 'sons of the prophets' in 2 Kings 2:3,5,7,15; 4:1,38; 5:22; 6:1 and 9:1?

3. Read Ezekiel 34:1-10. How did the 'shepherds of Israel' fail to 'take care of the flock'? 4. What is the biblical way of coping with unjust criticism (1 Cor. 4:2-5) and solving disputes (Matt. 18:15-17)? (See also Ps. 139:23-24; Heb. 4:12-13.)

TO THINK ABOUT AND DISCUSS

1. How can a Christian politician remain true to the Word of God? (Ps. 139:12-24; Amos 5:14; Rom. 2:6-11; Eph. 4:15.)

2. Are so-called 'white lies' ever justified? (See Ps. 15:2; Zech. 8:16; 2 Cor. 2:17; 4:2; Gal. 4:16; Eph. 4:25; Rev. 14:5.)

3. Can a person be 'called' into the work of the gospel without going to Bible or theological college? How can we decide whether a person is 'called' into such work of not?

13 Now is the time

(8:1-14)

Once again 'the Sovereign LORD' showed Amos a vision. At first glance this looked comforting; it was a basket of ripe fruit, such as we might give a visitor to the our homes or to someone recovering from an illness in hospital. In hot lands, such a gift is especially welcome because the moist, sweet flesh offers refreshment and sustenance. The fact that this fruit was ripe suggests the juiciness of produce that is ready and waiting to be eaten.

The over-ripe people of Israel (8:1-3)

However, this fruit symbolized that the people of Israel were ripe and ready to be consumed. As the fruit was ripe for eating, so were the people ripe for destruction. This is why God told the prophet, 'I will spare them no longer' (v. 3). In fact they were like over-ripe fruit—soft and flabby, infected with fungus, and fit for nothing but to be thrown into the rubbish bin.

Again the Lord speaks of 'that day' (v.3; see also 5:18). When the harvest was ripe the people celebrated 'The Feast of Tabernacles'. This feast was given to them as a reminder of the blessings of God's provision for them during their many years of wilderness wanderings. This time of rejoicing in the Old Testament was a period when the people looked back in gratitude for past deliverances and provision but it was also an occasion to look to the future and seek God's blessings for the year to come. 'It was, for God's people, the "turn of the year". ... The year had ripened and a new year stretched before them'.[26]

But this particular year that Amos wrote about was to be different. It was the people's wickedness that had ripened so that God would 'spare them no longer' (v.3). These are the same words that were spoken at the end of the vision of the plumb-line in 7:8. We see, then, that this would not be a temporary separation for a trial period. There is no suggestion that they would escape punishment if or when they repented. It is too late for that; their iniquity was full and they would soon be taken away into exile.

Amos goes on to describe the scene of 'that day': the songs in the temple would turn to wailing (v.3); the whole land would tremble and be stirred up and then sink again (v.8); the sun would set at noon and the earth would be dark at the time of bright daylight (v.9); their feasts would be turned into mourning and their singing would change into deep lamentation (v.10).

Amos graphically depicts the effect of the invading forces. There would be 'many, many bodies—flung everywhere!'

There would be cries of pain, howls of agony followed by 'Silence!' (v.3) but this silence would not speak about the end of their suffering; it would demonstrate the awful horror of God's judgement against sinners.

The reaction of the people to this vision (8:4-6)

We would expect the tragedy of such words to bring horror to the people, but instead there was only impatience—particularly from the rich people (the merchants) whose only desire was to continue growing richer. These did not cease to 'trample the needy and do away with the poor of the land' (v.4).

Instead of enjoying the religious feasts which had been given for the benefit of everyone, these merchants could hardly wait for them to be over so that they could get back to selling grain. But they did not only enjoy the profit that the market brought; they took delight in swindling the poor. Their dishonest scales boosted their profit by cheating their customers—'buying the poor with silver and the needy for a pair of sandals, selling even the sweepings with the wheat' (v.6). And they were doing this with a pretence of holiness. They pretended that they were enjoying the Sabbath days, but all the while they were eager to get on and make more money.

Striking contrasts of doom (8:7-10)

Once again the Lord swears by an oath. In 4:2 he had sworn by his holiness and in 6:8 by himself, but here he swears by 'the Pride of Jacob'. In Psalm 47:4 (and Isa. 58:14) the pride of Jacob refers to the people's inheritance (their land) but 'as this passage does not refer to the land it must be a title for God himself'.[27] As God never changes, the people of Israel could be assured that his word would never fail. He says, 'I will never forget anything that they have done'. Although they were God's chosen people, they had forfeited that privilege by refusing to reform their ways.

In verses 8-10 we are given a list of contrasting physical features. This is to demonstrate that the judgements destined for Israel were dramatic. Once again God's message, through his servant Amos, is unmistakable; these are not mere words that could be easily ignored.

> As God never changes, the people of Israel could be assured that his word would never fail. He says, 'I will never forget anything that they have done'. Although they were God's chosen people, they had forfeited that privilege by refusing to reform their ways.

Because the Lord would not forget anything that the people had done (in disregarding his laws), his anger would be demonstrated first of all by an earthquake. In 2:13, such an event caused a cart to crash and in 9:1 it was to 'strike the tops of the pillars [of the altar] so that the thresholds shake'.

God reminds the people of the annual flooding of the river Nile in Egypt. Because of the heavy seasonal rains in Ethiopia, the Nile rose by around twenty-five feet every year. That was a good thing because it brought large amounts of rich soil from the mountains and deposited it on the land.

However, the anger which the Lord would show on the northern kingdom of Israel would not bring blessing but punishment, as the earthquake would bring devastation upon the land (Amos uses similar language in 9:5).

Once again we are told that the day of the Lord would not bring light, but darkness (see 5:18, 20). Then, in verse 10, Amos focuses our attention upon the people, particularly those who claimed to be 'religious'. God would turn their joyous feasts into mourning and all their singing would be turned into weeping. We saw in 7:9 that their high places would be destroyed so it is not surprising that we next learn that they would put on the customary signs of mourning. God's actions would cause them to put off their normal clothing and instead adorn themselves with sackcloth and shave their heads.

I lost an eighteen-year-old son in a car crash some years ago, and I know, from personal experience, how grievous the loss of a son is. But I also took the funeral service of the only son of an elderly widowed lady who lives just a few doors away from me. She now has no child to care for her in her old age, and she is sad. Jeremiah records a similar event when he says, 'O my people, put on sackcloth and roll in ashes; mourn with bitter wailing as for an only son, for suddenly the destroyer will come upon us' (Jer. 6:26). It is no wonder that God's judgement will be like a bitter day (v.10).

The final judgement (8:11-14)

When I was young, no one told me that when I became old I would find certain actions difficult that I once did without thought. Now I find that walking up a hill is a bit of a strain, my knee joints sometimes ache, and I get tired much quicker than I used to do. Youth is similar to health; few appreciate it until it starts to leave them.

For many years the people of Israel had regarded those who preached God's word as a necessary nuisance. Sometimes they told the prophets not to speak (2:11-12) and even rejected Amos and his message (7:10-17). In this passage we find them thoroughly frightened and, at last, seeking for deliverance. They are so overcome with anxiety that they 'stagger from sea to sea and wander from north to east searching for the word of the Lord' (v.12). They are desperate, and want someone to hear their cries and come and help them.

They were just like so many today who want to have God at hand as a kind of 'insurance policy' only to be called upon on those occasions when they cannot cope on their own. In their panic, the people of Israel staggered around just like drunks (like those in Isa. 24:20), looking for help in every place they could think of.

Those who for most of their lives have rejected the Lord and his Word try all kinds of 'remedies' for their ills. They turn to the various 'New Age' trinkets, or to one of the cults; they look everywhere except to the one true and living God. The people of Amos's time looked from 'sea to sea' (i.e. from the Mediterranean to the Dead Sea) and from 'north to east' (from Dan to the Arabah). The one place where they did not go was to the south. There, in Jerusalem, was the one place where the light of God still shone. They tried everything else—except the truth.

In Amos 4:6-8 we read that the Lord had given the people

'empty stomachs in every city and lack of bread in every town.' He had also 'withheld rain from [them]' in an attempt to encourage them to return to him, but now something even more severe was to descend on them. There would be a famine, but this time it would not be of food or water; it would be a 'famine of hearing the words of the LORD' (v.11).

As before (e.g. in 4:6-8), 'the lovely young women and strong young men will faint because of thirst'. Young people who reject the faith of their parents may finally endeavour to seek help but will discover that they are overcome with a thirst arising from the lack of the word of the Lord. Their natural strength and beauty will not be sufficient for them in 'that day'.

When the people turned to the old gods of Samaria, Dan and Beersheba, they would discover that these would fail them. The people searched for 'spiritual help' among false gods because they had a 'depraved mind, to do what ought not to be done' (Rom. 1:28).

In the last chapter of the Bible John is told that 'the time is near'. Then, those who do wrong will continue to do wrong and those who are vile will continue to be vile (Rev. 22:10-11). In that day, there will be no further call to repentance because the age of grace will have outrun its course. The word of the Lord, which had often called people to leave their sin and turn to him, will be silent; and everyone whose name is 'not found written in the book of life [will be] thrown into the lake of fire' (Rev. 20:15).

FOR FURTHER STUDY

1. What are some of the blessings which God provides for his people? (See Ps. 65:11 and Ps. 118:25-28.)

2. Read Isaiah 47:5; Jeremiah 51:55 and Revelation 8:1. What is the significance of silence in these passages?

3. Although the Lord always forgives and receives those who truly repent of their sins, it is important to remember that he cannot overlook sin. Read Genesis 6:3 and 1 Peter 3:20: what are the consequences of man's sin in these verses?

4. Study Romans 1. What is man like in his 'depraved' state? Paul describes the last days as those in which children are 'disobedient to their parents'. What are the other signs of the last days in 2 Timothy 3:1-9?

TO THINK ABOUT AND DISCUSS

1. How can we best warn our friends about the danger they are in without Christ as their Saviour? (See Ezek. 3:20-21; 33:1-6; Luke 13:1-5; Acts 3:19.)

2. How can we explain to them what it would be like to live in a world without the influence of the Bible? (See 1 Sam. 3:1; 28:6 and 2 Chr. 15:3.)

14 God's action against the sinful kingdom

(9:1-10)

In this fifth and final vision (9:1-4) Amos tells us that he saw 'the Lord', rather than 'the Sovereign LORD' (as in 7:1).

This different word translated 'Lord' (Adonai) indicates that God is 'the one who rules over all';[28] this indicates that there is now a changed relationship between God and Israel. The whole of this section shows that there would be no hope of deliverance for Israel (apart from one glimmer of hope in verse 8). Israel's doom is sealed, because they persisted in their mistaken belief that as God's chosen people they could behave as they liked.

The destruction of the people (9:1-4)

In verse 1, Amos sees the Lord standing by the altar, just as Jeroboam I had stood by the altar 150 years before (1 Kings 12:32-33). He sees 'the Lord' in his mighty power, speaking with a powerful voice 'like the sound of rushing waters' (Rev. 1:15). We are not told whether it is an angel or God himself who is to 'strike the tops of the pillars', but certainly the destructive action comes from the Lord because in verses 1-4 he is telling Amos what he will do.

God is standing by the altar which is in a temple, perhaps one like that at Bethel in which the people had placed their hope of security. If that is the case then the Israelites must have been puzzled by these words. The more discerning among them would have trembled as his words roared out, 'Strike the tops of the pillars so that the thresholds shake' (v.1).

The pillars of the temple were the strong vertical beams that held up the roof of the building. If the tops of these pillars were struck with an extremely powerful blow then the thresholds of the temple would certainly shake and the pillars would fall.

In his vision Amos sees this temple filled with 'worshippers' who hoped that their ritual would bring God's blessing upon them. However, when the pillars collapsed, the whole structure would come down and kill them. As terrifying as this is, that is not the end. Even those who had escaped alive from the building would be hunted and slain with the sword. 'No one will get away, none will escape' (v.1). Those who expected security in that place would be disillusioned as they would discover that they are not able to hide from God's wrath.

It is God's hand (v.2), his 'eyes' (v.4) and his 'will' (mentioned all the way through vv.1-4) that would capture and destroy them. If they tried to escape by digging down to the depths of the grave (Sheol, the place of the departed), the hand of the Lord would reach down and bring them up for destruction, and the same hand will bring them down to earth should they should seek to climb up to the heavens.

This pictorial description is made more concrete in verses 3 and 4. In those days, the slopes of Mount Carmel were covered in thick woodland and littered with many caves, but if the people sought to hide in that mountain God would still 'hunt them down and seize them'. They would discover that, as the prophets of Baal found no escape from the sword of Elijah's supporters in that same place (1 Kings 18:40), they too would be hunted and put to death.

Those who dived into the depths of the sea and sought safety there from God's wrath would find none there either, because the Lord would send poisonous snakes to bite and kill them. Those 'driven into exile by their enemies' (v.4) would still be slain by the sword because God had 'fix[ed] his eye upon them for evil and not for good'. Just as the Lord had his eye upon his people for good (to protect and guide them— Deut. 32:10), so this same eye of God would be fixed on them, but this time for evil because of their wickedness. There will be no escape for those who persistently sin against the Lord and his law. God sees both gracious humility and blatant disobedience (see Ps. 139:7-12).

In praise of God's power (9:5-6)

As in a number of places in this prophecy, we now pause as Amos speaks (or sings) a hymn of praise to his God. He was not discouraged by the taunts of the people, whether they were rich or poor, insignificant or influential. Even the warnings of the priests did not cause him to hesitate in his work of bringing God's message to the people. So now he gave the people, and us today, these two verses which urge his hearers, and readers, to look up to the Lord.

This small section starts and ends with 'the LORD'. In case anyone has any doubts about the ability or willingness of God to carry out his threats, he tells us about this 'LORD', who is Almighty. God has only to touch 'the earth and it melts', bringing 'all who live in it [to] mourn'. He controls nature, because he not only made it, but orders it as well. As an example, Amos repeats what he said in 8:8, using the familiar illustration of the well-known annual flooding and receding of the Nile.

This God 'builds his lofty palace in the heavens' and 'sets its foundation on the earth'. Once again we are reminded that nothing is out of his sight or unknown to him. In verses 2-4 his power and his all-seeing eyes are referred to by telling us that no one can escape from him. He is everywhere around us. He can, and does, call 'for the waters of the sea and pours them out over the face of the land'. The destructive powers of even the greatest tsunamis are under his control.

But is not Israel God's chosen people? (9:7-10)

There was a special relationship between God and Israel but, as we have seen very many times, the sins of the people had broken that sacred chord. It is true that Israel was special. God had brought about a sovereign and mighty deliverance for them in saving them from the grip of the Egyptians. This was a tremendous act of love on behalf of the children of Israel which they had never forgotten. But their remembrance of this had not served to prick their consciences. They had not ceased from their sinning, nor did they return to the Lord.

The prophet then reminds these disobedient people that Israel is not the only nation that God has moved from one place to another. It must have been a crushing rebuke for the self-satisfied 'super-spiritual' people of Israel to be told, 'Are not you Israelites the same to me as the Cushites?' (v.7). The Cushites came from the Upper Nile (the southern part of Egypt), and some scholars believe that they were the Ethiopians referred to in Jeremiah 13:23. We do not know why these Cushites were mentioned at this point. Perhaps it was just because they lived far, far away and the Lord wanted Israel to know that he cared for people who were at a distance in the same way that he had his eye upon those who were near.

> It must have been a crushing rebuke for the self-satisfied 'super-spiritual' people of Israel to be told, 'Are not you Israelites the same to me as the Cushites?'

But the other two nations whom the Lord speaks of are two of their near neighbours, and their bitterest of enemies. How can it be that the Lord can lump Israel together with these heathen people? It was because he not only brought Israel up from Egypt, he also brought the Philistines from Caphtor (Crete) and the Arameans (Syrians) from Kir, an unidentified place which is possibly the one to which the Arameans would return (see 1:5).

But there is a further, more serious sense in which Israel is the same as these heathen nations. Israel, God's chosen people, had become like these others in that they had cut themselves off from God through their disobedience. Amos had constantly been telling them this, but they were deaf to his pleas. The qualification for being the sons of Israel was faith in God and obedience to his laws. On both of these counts they had failed, as Amos would show them in the following verses.

It is sad when people know the way they ought to behave but become so complacent that they are unaware that they have strayed from the right pathway. If a nation, or an individual, persists in sinful ways then soon the conscience will be numbed and lawlessness will follow. In Amos 6:1 and 13, the prophet had warned the Israelites not to place their hope of security on the fact that God had saved them in the past. He urged them to do good and not drift along in a complacent haze.

Truly born-again people have been saved with an everlasting salvation. We have been saved from the wrath to come (Rom. 2:5 and Rev. 6:17), but we have no excuse for slack behaviour. We must constantly strive to 'throw off … the sin that easily entangles [us]' (Heb. 12:1) and seek to live pure and holy lives.

The proud Israelites, who would have been shocked to hear that God regarded these surrounding nations in the same way as he thought of them, would have been even more horrified to learn that the 'eyes of the Sovereign LORD are on the sinful kingdom' (v.8). Who is this 'sinful kingdom'? It is these very people who had trusted that all was well with them. Can you imagine the incredulous look on their faces as Amos told them that God said, 'I will destroy it [the sinful kingdom] from the face of the earth'? Certainly 'The eyes of the LORD are on the righteous and his ears are attentive to their cry' (Ps. 34:15). However, 'The face of the LORD is against those who do evil, to cut off the memory of them from the earth' (Ps. 34:16).

But then comes this one small glimmer of hope. Amos adds, almost in a whisper so that only the discerning will hear it, 'yet I will not totally destroy the house of Jacob' (v.8). There will be a remnant saved who have not indulged in the sin of the majority of the Israelites. Isaiah was to speak of this comparatively small group of people who would remain faithful to the Lord as 'a shoot' coming up 'from the stump of Jesse' (Isa. 11:1).

One of the effects of God shaking the house of Israel (v.9) is that those who have not been diverted from the truth will be sieved out. As grain is placed in a sieve and shaken to allow the dust, dirt and husks to fall to the ground and be swept up with the rubbish, so Israel will be shaken at God's command and those precious pebbles of God's holy grain (faithful believers) will be saved. They will not reach the ground and be destroyed.

However, all sinners among God's people will die by the sword—even those who feel secure, saying, 'Disaster will not overtake or meet us, because we are God's chosen people.'

FOR FURTHER STUDY

1. Study Psalm 139. What are the differences between those who seek to be pure before God (vv.23-24) and those who try to run away from God's judgement and refuse to 'seek the LORD and live' (Amos 5:6)?

2. What are the wonders of God on which Amos reflects in his pauses in this prophecy? See 4:13; 5:8-9 and 9:5-6.

3. Study Ephesians 2:11-18. What are the different ways in which God has brought us peace?

TO THINK ABOUT AND DISCUSS

1. How can we help people to understand that our God is not only approachable, loving and forgiving, but that he is also a powerful Lord who created and controls everything, and is so holy that he cannot look upon sin? (See Deut. 32:4; Ps. 46; Isa. 45:20-25; Hab. 1:12-17; Heb. 12:29; Rev. 5:1-10.)

2. Why does God allow disasters such as the Asian tsunami of 26 December 2004 to happen? (See Num. 16:28-34; Deut. 10:16-17; Rom. 8:28; Col. 1:16-17.)

3. What happens when the conscience is suppressed? (See Exod. 7-11; Rom. 1:24-28; Eph. 4:19; 1 Tim. 4:2.)

4. How, and why, should our behaviour reflect God's holiness? (Study 1 Peter 1:13-22.)

15 The promise of Israel's restoration

(9:11-15)

After all of the gloom and despondency of much of the earlier part of Amos, we now come to extreme joy as we see the unfolding of God's promise of great blessing for those who are faithful to him and his word.

Five wonderful promises (9:11-12)

Once again we read about 'that day'. For the remnant, those who sincerely follow the Lord (the ones who are 'called by his name'— 2 Chron. 7:14), there will be great blessing. The dire warnings of judgement will pass them by because God is gracious and he will have mercy on those who honour him and his word.

However, these blessings will not come about as a reward because of what the people do; they will happen because the Lord acts to bring blessing on the people who are faithful to his word.

In the days in which Amos prophesied, the dynasty of King David was in ruins (soon the temple at Jerusalem would also be destroyed) and the surrounding nations continually opposed God's chosen people. 'That day' would not only be a time when these nations would be judged but it would also usher in a time when the faithful remnant would be blessed. There are five things that the Lord himself says he will do: 'I will restore'; 'I will repair'; [I will] restore' (again); '[I will] build'; and '[I will] do these things'.

The first thing that God will do is 'restore David's fallen tent'. This word 'tent' could be translated 'hut' or 'booth'. Before David built his temple at Jerusalem, the ark lived in a tabernacle, a tent. In saying that David's tent had fallen, Amos was emphasizing that the rule of King David had crumbled. Throughout this prophecy he had been pointing out to the people that the influence of godly King David's reign had withered away. The evidence that Amos had given for this was the state of the land.

The people had had ample opportunities to start to put these matters right, but they had done nothing to restore righteousness. However, God was going to do things! He was going to bring judgement 'in that day'. He would 'restore David's fallen tent' and set it upright again. He would repair its broken places. He would restore its ruins and he would build it as it used to be. There would be a restoration of Israel and David's kingdom, a kingdom that would have no end.

Verse 12 tells us why God is going to do this: this kingdom will 'possess the remnant of Edom and all the nations that bear [his] name'. The faithful people of God will be possessed not by cruel attack, but by a loving Father. Those who serve the Lord are his willing slaves; their joy is to be servants of Jesus Christ, as Paul often described himself.

Edom had already been mentioned in 2:11 as a nation reserved for God's wrath. Throughout their history Israel had suffered from unhelpfulness and downright hostility particularly from the proud people of Edom. They lived high up in their rocky abode and behaved as though they were far superior to anyone else. At one time, David's kingdom had included many of the surrounding nations and even Edom had been conquered by his armies (see 2 Sam. 8:14), a feat which no other nation had accomplished. But why does God say that the house of David will possess (or own) the remnant of Edom, when it has clearly been stated that in 'that day' Edom will be utterly destroyed (Obad. 18)? The answer must surely be that 'on Mount Zion' there was deliverance (Obad. 17) and as with Israel, a faithful remnant of the people would flee to Mount Zion (Christ) for this deliverance.

Verse 12 outlines the glorious missionary expansion of the church. Abraham had been promised that he would be the father of 'many nations' (Gen. 17:4), and these nations would include Gentile as well as Jewish peoples. We can know for certain what this verse means because James quotes this passage in his speech at the Jerusalem Council in Acts 15:16-17. He uses this as evidence that the Gentiles must be included and welcomed into the church of Jesus Christ.

How will this expansion of God's people take place? By the powerful action of God, who will send out his messengers into all the nations to call out a people for himself (1 Peter 2:9). They will take to the ends of the earth the message of salvation by grace through faith alone, and all who believe will be willingly possessed by God.

The powerful effect of God's promises (9:13-15)

Because God has promised blessing, it will surely come, but the time of its coming is not specified. The people will have to watch and wait. Just as those of Old Testament times waited for the coming Messiah, so God's people today wait for the return of the Lord Jesus Christ. Some of the messianic promises in the Old Testament refer to the birth of the Lord Jesus at Bethlehem and some of them have to do with his final return in judgement upon this earth. The Lord does not keep us waiting in order to tease us; he wants us to be ready at whatever time he may come. We know that the blessings of these final verses of Amos have not yet arrived. They surely speak of a restoration of all things—a time when sin and injustice will have been banished and the reign of righteousness will cover the whole earth.

> Because God has promised blessing, it will surely come, but the time of its coming is not specified. The people will have to watch and wait. Just as those of Old Testament times waited for the coming Messiah, so God's people today wait for the return of the Lord Jesus Christ.

Verse 13 speaks of material prosperity. For the people of Amos's day, this meant agricultural prosperity. He prophesies that a time of abundant harvest would come: so much, that the reapers would still be gathering it in when the ploughman came to start getting the ground ready for the next planting of seed. And the juice from the grapes, used to make new wine, would be so abundant that it would seem like the mountains were dripping with the vast quantities of it. This is what the Lord had promised the young nation of Israel in Leviticus 26:3-5. However, the Lord had told them that this would only occur if the people 'follow my decrees and are careful to obey my commands'. Obviously they had not done this, but in a land where Christ reigns supreme, these wonderful provisions would be theirs.

> When Adam and Eve were banished from the Garden of Eden, a curse was put upon the land, but now that curse has been removed and a restored Eden will be re-established once again.

When Adam and Eve were banished from the Garden of Eden, a curse was put upon the land (Gen. 3:17-19), but now that curse has been removed and a restored Eden will be re-established once again. From this side of the cross we know that the curse of sin can be washed away only by the shedding of the precious blood of a sinless man. We know that, through Christ's atoning death, sin has been removed; and one day he will reign supremely on this earth because Satan and all his evil hosts will have been banished from it.

In verse 14 we have a different picture, but one depicting the same event. This verse tells us about the enjoyment of the people who will dwell in the land. It is a complete reversal of what was stated in 5:11. There the people would not live in the stone mansions that they had built, nor drink wine from the lush vineyards they had planted. But 'the days are coming' when God will bring back his exiled people Israel and they will rebuild the ruined cities and live in them. They will plant vineyards and drink their wine; and they will make gardens and eat their fruit.

God now calls the remnant 'my people'. Once (in the days of their sinfulness) they were 'not my people' but now (in the restored Eden) they 'are the people of God' (1 Peter 2:10). The Lord had declared that he would destroy the sinful kingdom from the face of the earth (v.8), so those whom God will 'bring back' to the land are obviously those who have repented of their sins and been cleansed from them.

The final verse of this prophecy speaks about God's action in planting Israel in their own land. Some believe that this verse and Romans 11 speak of a coming time when the present-day nation of Israel will return to the Lord and be planted securely in their own territory. However, there is a spiritual meaning here that applies to Jew and Gentile alike. All believers in the Lord Jesus Christ are God's Israel (1 Peter 2:4-10). They will never be uprooted from the land God has given to them. That land

> All believers in the Lord Jesus Christ are God's Israel (1 Peter 2:4-10). They will never be uprooted from the land God has given to them. That land is heaven and glory.

is heaven and glory. How do we know that these things are true? We can be certain because it is the word of 'the LORD your God' (v. 15).

Some scholars seek to bring doubt upon the genuineness of these last verses in the prophecy of Amos; they cannot understand how they can be so different from the rest of the book. But those who have ears to hear will hear what God is saying to them in these days, and he will bring great blessing on all those who read, hear and obey.

FOR FURTHER STUDY

1. Read Jeremiah 30:9-11, John 5:24-29 and Romans 2:6-10. What will happen on 'that day'?

2. Read Genesis 17:4 and God's promise to Abraham. How do we see this promise worked out through the Bible? (See Gen. 17:4; Rom. 4:16-8; 15:8-12; Gal. 3:29; Rev. 7:9; 21:24.)

3. Study the Parable of the Ten Virgins in Matthew 25:1-13. How can God's people today make sure they are ready for his coming?

4. What will the coming age be like, when Christ reigns supremely in justice? (See Num. 14:21; Isa. 11:1-16; Hab. 2:14; Rev. 21:1-14.)

TO THINK ABOUT AND DISCUSS

1. What should our attitude be towards those who are not Christians? (See Matt. 28:18-20; Rom. 10:14-15.)

2. How can the church conquer the nations? (See 2 Cor. 10:3-6; Gal. 3:26-29; Eph. 1:20-23.)

3. What should be the Christian's attitude towards the Second Coming of the Lord? How should the knowledge of this affect the way that we live? (See 1 Cor. 1:7 and 2 Peter 3:10-13.)

Endnotes

1 NIV Study Bible, Hodder and Stoughton, 1987, p.1324.

2 Quoted by John Blanchard in *Where was God on September 11th?*, Evangelical Press, 2002.

3 NIV Study Bible, p.1326.

4 Gordon J. Keddie, *The Lord is his name*, Evangelical Press, 1986, p.20.

5 As above, p.23.

6 Lloyd J. Ogilvie in *The Communicator's Commentary—Hosea, Joel, Amos, Obadiah, Jonah*, Word Publishers, 1990, p.283.

7 Keddie, p.33.

8 As above, p.44.

9 As above, p.50.

10 As above, p.53.

11 Gary V. Smith, The NIV Application Commentary on Hosea/Amos/Micah, Zondervan, 2001, p.170.

12 Keddie, p.59.

13 Smith, p.177.

14 As above, p.222.

15 As above, p.233.

16 Ray Beeley, *Roaring of the Lion: Amos*, Banner of Truth Trust, 1969, p.72.

17 As above, p.72.

18 J. Van de Venter, All to Jesus I surrender.

19 Smith, p.254.

20 By Carl Sigman & Herb Magidson. Recorded by Guy Lombardo, 1950.

21 Ogilvie, p.326.

22 As above, p.330.

23 Roger Ellsworth, *The God of all comfort*, Evangelical Press, 2004, p.160.

24 Beeley, p.90.

25 Smith, p.269.

26 Keddie, p. 111.

27 Smith, p.343.

28 Keddie, p. 120.

The
Opening
up
series

Opening up
Exodus

Opening up
Ezra

Opening up
Psalms

Opening up
Ecclesiastes

Opening up
Ezekiel's visions

Opening up
Amos

Opening up
Nahum

Opening up
1 Corinthians

Further
titles in
preparation

Opening up
Philippians

Opening up
1 Thessalonians

Opening up
1 Timothy

Opening up
2 & 3 John

This fine series is aimed at the 'average person in the church' and combines brevity, accuracy and readability with an attractive page layout. Thought-provoking questions make the books ideal for both personal or small group use.

'Laden with insightful quotes and penetrating practical application, Opening up Philippians is a Bible study tool which belongs on every Christian's bookshelf!'

DR. PHIL ROBERTS, PRESIDENT, MIDWESTERN BAPTIST THEOLOGICAL SEMINARY, KANSAS CITY, M I S S O U R I

Please contact us for a free catalogue

In the UK ☎ 01568 613 740   **email—** sales@dayone.co.uk

In the United States: ☎ Toll Free: 1-8-morebooks

In Canada: ☎ 519 763 0339 www.dayone.co.uk